STORYTELLING—
IT'S EASY!

STORYTELLING—
IT'S EASY!

By

ETHEL BARRETT

ZONDERVAN
PUBLISHING HOUSE OF THE ZONDERVAN CORPORATION
GRAND RAPIDS, MICHIGAN 49506

ISBN 0-310-20561-1

Printed in the United States of America

83   84   85   86   87   88 — 30   29   28   27   26

To my favorite audience

GARY AND STEVE

and

TO MY MOTHER

who always spurred me on

Table Of Contents

Table Of Contents

Introduction

Most failure in front of audiences is not because of inability but because of a lack of knowledge of surprisingly practical things. The technical know-how we can get in textbooks; the practical know-how is harder to come by.

This book is an attempt to provide some of the help we need in storytelling and all its ramifications, in the classroom and on the platform. Part of it evolved from background material written for lectures; the rest of it evolved as a result of a myriad of questions asked me by students down through the years, disclosing that platform people have problems that are not always solved in academic textbooks. The questions filled a notebook but basic patterns emerged—the desire to probe beyond the theory, to understand the psychology and etiquette of the speaker-audience relationship, to know how to cope with the multitude of unseen pitfalls that can sabotage an otherwise good presentation, and to discover the extra "intangibles" that lift the passably-good presentation out of the realm of mediocrity. Though many of these pages are of necessity devoted to the technicalities of rhetoric and dramatics—most of them are extremely practical and experiential; I have tried not to traffic in unfelt or unproved truths. The instructions given with such authority are reliable for I have tried them and know they work. The reality of the pitfalls spoken of so glibly I vouch for because I have fallen into them.

It is written for both storytellers and speakers—for many storytellers get to be speakers—and every speaker should be versed in the art of storytelling. It is written for teachers, both Sunday school and secular—for down through the ages some of the greatest teachers have used this method to cement their points in the minds of their listeners. And for men as well as women—for the idea that a person who tells stories must be a woman is a myth that the men themselves have exploded. They have invaded the field of storytelling and are here to stay. These are the days when more and more men are gleefully teaching primary and pre-school in Sunday schools across the nation with, I might add, phenomenal success. And why not? They make superb storytellers. They have better built-in vocal equipment to begin with. Their voices are more versatile. A man can, by using a stage whisper with a little sound in it, simulate the voice of a woman, a small boy, even a little girl. A woman is not so fortunate in imitating the masculine voices. She might do well as a booming giant, but she has a hard time being convincing as an ordinary man.

Because the contents have been concerned with the message, preliminaries have been mentioned only in passing, and only when they had a direct bearing on the speaker. This is not because they are unimportant, but because they fall in another category and have no place in this discourse. It might do well to mention here that they play a vital role in the program. Shuffling about and talking during preliminaries as if the program "hadn't really started yet" is to be deplored. I have the greatest respect for them, perhaps because it was during preliminaries that I was once brought up short by a line in a song—to face one of the most important decisions of my life. The words rang in my mind all the rest of the evening, and I never heard the speaker! The speaker, however, is the one we are concerned about here.

Perhaps a word of explanation regarding the anecdotal material is in order. At first fictitious names were used in all of the personal illustrations to avoid the appalling frequency of "I". The elimination of this evil, however, gave rise to another—the illustrations somehow lost their authenticity. It would be small comfort to the reader to know that some theoretical Mr. Brown had overcome this obstacle or Miss Smith had learned from that blunder. He might even be tempted to think it had been invented just for the purpose of proving a point. The author is not a psychologist or a doctor who can illustrate with case histories, leaving himself out of it.

So, at the last, it became somewhat autobiographical—for if it is true that we learn from mistakes—the person I have learned the most from is myself.

Read it as a guide-book—and remember that every guide-post was put there after years of tripping over microphone cords, falling on and off platforms, and facing every kind of audience from enthusiastic to gelid. My education in the "intangibles" has been empirical. I found out the hard way that storytelling could be easy. I hope that what I have learned and set down will make it easy for you.

STORYTELLING—
IT'S EASY!

Chapter 1

What, Why and Who

What Is Storytelling?

Back in the days when school busses were unheard of and we walked two miles along a country road to school—until my mother learned to drive a Model T by reading the book of instructions—we had, in English class, a peculiar form of torture known as "expression." There was never time to indulge in one pupil for long, and the harried teacher would have us come to the front of the room by turns and say four lines apiece of whatever bit of prose or poetry we were dissecting at the moment.

Most of what we learned there has gone underground into my subconscious—but I shall never forget one spring morning and the agony of us all, as we suffered vicariously with one boy who definitely did not have Thespian proclivities.

We were reciting "The Village Blacksmith"—four lines apiece. He sat across from me and I could see his lips move as he did the count-down, figuring out ahead which four lines would be his when his turn came, and hoping the bell would ring before it did. Time marched on inexorably, and he was at last in front of the room. He hitched his trousers, fixed his eyes on the horse-chestnut tree outside the window, took a long breath—and began.

"His hair was thick and black and long
His face was like the tan.
He looked the whole world IN the face—
F'reowed not any man."

"Sammy." The teacher was grim but patient. This was not going to be easy. "Try it again. And don't gallop so. You sound like an eccentric wheel off-center. He looked the WHOLE WORLD in the face."

"Yes'm."

We waited expectantly.

"His hair was thick and black and long.
His face was like the tan.
He looked the whole world IN the face—"

"Sammy. Not 'Didup didup didUP didup! There's a thought behind it. He doesn't owe anybody anything—not even Sears Roebuck. It's a wonderful feeling. He looks the WHOLE WORLD in the face. Do you see?"

"Yes'm."

"Try it. Just the last two lines. 'He looks the WHOLE WORLD in the face.' "

We strained forward, mentally helping him. He shifted to the other foot.

"He looks the whole world IN the fa— . . .
Yes'm?"

"I—didn't say anything."

"Yes'm. But you looked kinda funny."

"Sammy—take your seat. And write the poem. I'll mark you on punctuation." She knew when she was licked.

Sammy, we concluded, didn't have it. It was like being tone-deaf and having the teacher blow

on her pitch-pipe, and the pupil singing

with his voice. He can't sing it because he can't hear it, and he can't hear it because he doesn't have the gift of pitch, any more than Sammy had the gift of expression.

And that is what storytelling is.

It's a gift. The ability to tell a story well is the gift of expression, the gift of interpretation—the ability to take an event from the memory or from the printed page—and make it come to life.

Just as few people are tone-deaf, few people are totally without this gift. It is lying dormant within most of us, buried under inhibitions and inaction. We are either afraid, or have never taken the time to do anything about it.

Gifts can be developed and brought to perfection only

by labor and know-how and study. God has told us to "stir up the gifts that are in us"—to use our talents. Of all talents, the ability to tell stories is one of the most useful—and the most exciting.

It's a ministry. Storytelling is a means of reaching "children of all ages" with the good things of God. You are not limited; you have vast possibilities in a story that you will never have in a speech. And if your forte is lessons or sermons or speeches, you have limitless opportunities to apply your storytelling know-how to your illustrations. People remember a story. They also remember the illustrations long after they've forgotten the speaker. Spurgeon once said that illustrations were like windows, letting the light stream in. Storytelling is vivid, bringing to life before the listener things that might never have been real to him before.

It's a message. At least it should be. A message wrapped up in an attractive package, easily assimilated and digested.

It's painting a picture of people and things, events and happenings. As such, it must have the lights and shadows of a good picture, the contrast, the appeal. It must tell something, picture something. It must produce an effect.

It's work. In radio and television, the consensus is that a program takes an hour of work for a minute of finished time. It is more than just assimilating a few facts and telling them into a story. It requires a knowledge of dramatics, of writing, of audience types and demands, of psychology and people. But it's "fun" work. Everything we are going to talk about in this book is fun. And what is fun, is easy!

What, Why And Who

Why We Learn To Do It

The best reason for learning something about storytelling is that glibness isn't always reliable. Without preparation and know-how, sooner or later it will trip you up. You should be able to stand on your feet and say your say with credit. If you are glib, you can be a fairly good storyteller, or even a good one—but if you have any talent at all, you owe it to yourself to be an extraordinary one.

In learning the finer intricacies of the art, you can lift yourself right out of the realm of mediocrity and really compensate listeners for their trouble to listen. *Give them their time's worth!* Why be just good when you can be best? Those most at home on the platform or before a class are the ones who prepared the hardest and who never begin without a bit of knee-shaking.

Who Can Do It

Personality-wise, the best storytellers are those who like people. Listeners cannot warm up to a person who stands aloof and speaks to them from across a great gulf, no matter how well he is prepared. They like a speaker who likes THEM. If this seems oversimplified, remember, there ARE speakers who love *humanity* and hate *people*. A missionary wrote home once, "Everything is fine here—except for these natives."

You are not telling stories for the sake of telling stories. You are telling stories to people. Fall in love with your audience. They love you, or they would not be there. The least you can do is love them back.

We conclude, then, that storytelling is a gift lying dormant in almost everybody and almost certainly lying dormant in you. It is fun, and anything that is fun is easy. And unless you hate people—you can do it!

There are three essentials to the success of a story.

1. You
2. The Story
3. The Audience

If you can control the first two, it follows that, all things being equal, you will control the third.

Now let's do it.

Chapter 2

You

The Little Man

Of course a combination of a number of faculties are necessary to do almost anything, but all things being equal, a boxer uses his biceps, a scientist uses his mind, a proofreader uses his eyes. You, in speaking use your nervous system. Not per se. You have used your brain and prayers in preparation—but in the last analysis, the drain is on your nerves.

If listening consumes nervous energy, speaking certainly consumes more. The consumption is relative, depending on your material and your audience.

Russell Conwell, preacher of the famed "Acres of Diamonds," used to say that if a speech of his went well, he would go home feeling exhilarated; if it went poorly, he would go home feeling as if he'd been horse-whipped. Although it is more rewarding to go home feeling exhilarated—in either case, the drain is there. It is there both in neophytes and hierophants. In the beginner it takes the form of real fear. In the experienced speaker it settles down to a feeling of responsibility to the audience that came out to hear him. It is this feeling of responsibility that makes the good speaker expend the same effort on his two thousandth presentation that he did on the first. He knows he is fallible and the fact that his first one thousand nine hundred and ninety-nine presentations were successful does not guarantee this one will be. It is possible that Russell Conwell's "Acres of Diamonds" would not have been preached so often and so successfully if Conwell had not realized this. The good speaker expects to be drained. If he is not drained, he is worried. If he is not worried, he is slipping.

But what of the neophyte? What of the nervousness and real fear that plagues him in the beginning? And how to conquer it?

What makes it difficult is that it is one of those things you cannot put your finger on. The part of your nervous system that is affected is the part over which you have no direct control. It is known both as your involuntary nervous system and your parasympathetic nervous system. By any name it is a bugaboo.

I have often suspected that there is a little man down inside each of us, somewhere in that nervous system, sitting at a switchboard, hatching plots of mischief, amusing himself at our expense.

You have to tell a story? He plugs in and . . .

"Hello. Is this the adrenalin department? Well, dump a pint in her bloodstream. Right away. Before she gets on the platform." And you are off like a rocket—all hands, no tongue, all chattering knees and teeth.

You have to speak to the whole department? Ah, that is his delight, the epitome of his amusement.

"Hello. The saliva department? Well, turn it off. I don't want him to have a drop to swallow."

And you can see where you are. Right where he wants you. You cannot conceal the results of his mischief. There is no use trying to look at ease when your hands are clammy and trembling

and your throat is dry. You cannot conceal nervousness—you have to conquer it.

Something must be done.

The boxer trains and coddles his biceps—the
scientist trains his mind—the proofreader takes
care of his eyes. But how to coddle a system over
which you have no direct control. It is not easy.

But it is possible after a fashion. You DO have
remote control.

That little man has more or less authority at
the switchboard, depending on your degree of
tension. And you can, to a considerable extent,
lessen his ability to turn off the saliva. Obviously,
the more adept you become at speaking the less
switchboard interference you will have.

But how to begin?

There are few subjects duller than the things about
yourself you must now face. Posture, for instance. And
voice. And appearance. But face them you must, if you
would begin. And face up with alacrity. They have more
to do with that little man than you suspect. And meeting
them head-on will reward you in rich dividends.

Your Dress

Son number two came home one fall from his annual
summer camping spree with a pair of antlers that had once
been the pride of some buck who, judging by their size,
certainly must have been an undisputed paterfamilias. He
went to bed exhausted and very happy and left them on
the downstairs hall desk. The next morning as I went to
call him for breakfast, they caught my eye. I couldn't resist the impulse. I held them up to the sides of my head
and called up the stairs—"Steve—breakfast!"

As he appeared at the head of the stairs, the expression

on his face was something to behold. The antlers he knew, and his mother he knew—but his mother with antlers!

Definitely out of place.

The Supreme Court has gone on record as saying that a nuisance may be nothing more than *the right thing in the wrong place*. That is as good a rule as any to go by. If you are a woman and a lover of fancy hats—enjoy them by all means. But leave them on the shelf when you go in to teach. Don't face a group of small children with a hat that has a pendulum on it swinging from lofty heights. You can hypnotize people that way! On the platform you may wear them or not, depending on your presentation. If it is a story, the hat should be sacrificed to your art. I am a designers' sale addict myself—but not in the classroom or on the platform.

If you are a man and enjoying the long over-due emancipation of men's clothing from drab monotony to colorful sports coats, fancy vests and gorgeously gay leisure shirts, wear them with propriety and be grateful that the men's clothing designers have at last enabled you to emerge from the cocoon. But remember that for the speaker they have not as yet replaced the conservative suit.

From your hat to your toes the same rule applies. Only a comedian may dress eccentrically. Your dress should be conservative—in good taste—suited to the occasion. Simplicity is the keynote of all good design and that includes clothing.

Are you teaching Sunday school? Dress for the occasion. Is your speaking further afield? The same rule applies. Inquire ahead if it is formal. I forgot to once, and showed up in a suit at a formal affair in a fashionable church in Boston. I have never forgotten my embarrassment. Nor have I ever made the same mistake again.

Dressing conservatively does not mean being colorless

or unattractive. On the contrary! It behooves you to be as attractive as you can!

Your Grooming

Anyone—expensively dressed or no—can be neatly groomed. It is expected, and justifiably so. Careless grooming will detract from the most carefully prepared—the most exquisitely delivered presentation. There are brushes and polishes and steam-irons. Remember you are for the moment on exhibition. The aids that keep you *nice to be near* are legion. Remember that in speaking your metabolism shoots up; it has the same effect on your body as hard physical exercise. So be *nice to look at* and *nice to be near* —and here again, be as attractive as you can.

God gave the mountains sky-tossed peaks and flanked the lakes with forest-green and gave the spring the breath-taking beauty of a dogwood tree. He squanders beauty everywhere—He is known for His extravagance and His meticulous attention to detail. He wants His children to at least look presentable.

Your Posture

It's a little thing, it is true. But life is made up of little things, and success in anything depends on the attention you give to little things, the minor details.

We were slouched happily over our pot roast dinner one night when son number two announced suddenly, apropos of nothing: "We had posture at cub scouts today."

Without anyones' telling anyone to—we straightened up to a man—and when I adjourned to the kitchen to bring dessert, I walked like a model practicing with a book on her head. The very word "posture" had snapped us to attention like the crack of a whip.

There are a number of things that begin with, or are

dependent upon, good posture. Your general appearance, your breath-control, your voice, to name a few. Good posture means good control of your body.

How to get it?

Try this:

> Stand erect with your head up, as though it were lifted by a wire from above, like a puppet.
>
> Lift your shoulders the least bit—as if the puppet-strings had been drawn slightly taught. Your hips should be slightly back, your knees drawn in and your legs straight. Keep your weight on the soles of your feet—one foot slightly ahead of the other.
>
> Two don'ts: Don't settle down on your heels. And don't let your knees sag!

Got it?

Now keep it. Practice it. Remind yourself of it. And keep at it until it becomes second nature. Like anything worth accomplishing, good posture is developed by keeping everlastingly at it. The results will be eminently worth while. When you speak or teach on your feet you will stand UP, not slouch over a table. When you teach from a chair, you will sit UP—not slouch forward. And your lungs will have a chance to expand. Many things that are "right" or "good for us" either taste dreadful or make us feel or look odd. This is the exception. You will actually look better. You will look relaxed because you will *be* relaxed. It is a "disciplined relaxation"—a result of good control. Good posture means good control.

Your Gestures

Now of course, with your posture under control, there is very little to say about gestures; they will just naturally take care of themselves. The question of "What'll I do with my hands?" just won't come up.

You

When you are completely relaxed, when you get to the point where you don't think about them—then you may do as you please with them. But because you want to—not because you don't know what to do with them. Until you reach that point, keep your hands hanging loosely at your sides!

Gone are the days when we learned a studied gesture to express each thought. I can still hear my mother saying, "Ethel, do your reading for the company—the one you learned last week." And I, right foot well forward, toe pointed, would begin. Every voice intonation, every gesture—was the result of careful study. And every thought had a gesture to go with it. I was the last word in authority on the matter. No one thought to question my methods, nor did it occur to anyone that I was ridiculous. I took "elocution" lessons!

But that form of speaking is gone, along with the lace tablecloth folded back of an evening to make room for homework along with the crystal set—along with my childhood.

And now, as we said, we do "what comes naturally." Within reason. The restrictions are few and very simple.

Don't over-do. If you are the ebullient type—and letting your gestures take care of themselves means constantly waving your arms akimbo and gesticulating wildly—you are in for a little discipline. Take yourself in hand.

Don't become addicted to one gesture. Here is where a best-friend-and-severest-critic is needed, as the addicts are seldom able to diagnose themselves. Ask someone to watch you—and tell you if you are constantly repeating the same gesture to the point of distraction. Then do something about stopping it. Just having it brought to your attention is often enough.

Don't become known for eccentric gestures. We had a professor once who was beloved by all; he was a wit and a charmer. But he had one gesture that embedded him in our memories in caricature for evermore. Every time he made a point he drew a little imaginary circle with his index finger and poked a point in the center of it. I have seen five hundred students in chapel watching that man, their eyes periodically rolling with him as he drew his circle, heads almost imperceptibly jutting forward as he poked in his point. He seemed utterly unaware of what he was doing, and we watched him with fond affection, not minding it really. But I am afraid that while he was poking the point in his imaginary circle, many a point was lost in his lecture.

There is no serious harm in an eccentric gesture except that an audience gets to watch for it—either with glee or with horrible fascination, depending on what it is. So the safest thing to do is—be done with it!

Gestures and posture go together and depend upon and affect each other. When you have mastered the "disciplined relaxation" that is the result of good control, you will have automatically mastered your gestures also. They will go along with the story, unaffected and unafraid. And you will forget to think, "What'll I do with my hands?"

Your Poise

The over-all result of all these practical things is that seemingly magic and intangible quality—poise.

It is as hard to pin down as quicksilver—as elusive as the last pea on a plate. We connect it with charm school, attribute it to only the chosen few—spin webs of mystery around it—do everything with it but get ahold of it. It is really a very practical quality. In fact, if you are diligently tackling the things in this chapter you are well on your way toward having it.

Poise is not art or studied gestures. It is not imitation. It is not affectation. It is something infinitely deeper. It is the ability—not only to be at ease when things are running smoothly—but to keep your head and come up unruffled when things are not.

One of our congressmen was speaking one night at a huge open-air meeting. Just above his head and slightly in front of him was a very bright light. His audience numbered in the thousands. The bugs flying around that light did, too. Everytime he leaned forward and drew in his breath to make a point, he came so alarmingly close to those flying bugs that the audience, to a man, began to think the same thought. And finally, that which they had feared—came upon him.

He leaned forward during a dramatic pause—took a deep breath, ready for his next point, and by the expression on his face, they knew the worst had happened. Now it was just a question of which throat the bug had gone down, and whether the speaker would be asphyxiated or finish the bug off by swallowing him. As he struggled, everyone held his breath with him, waiting for the denouement.

Then he swallowed and began to breathe again. So did everyone else. But did he forget his point? He did not! He leaned forward and with a menacing grin, said, "It served him right; he should have looked where he was going." And went on with his speech. He had poise.

When you can act at ease and look at ease because you ARE at ease—you have poise. It is as simple as that.

Confidence and Humility

It seems incongruous to speak of confidence and humility in the same breath; at first glance they would appear to be the antithesis of each other. If you have confidence, how in the name of common sense can you be humble? And is it not a bit unseemly, *if not downright unspiritual*, to be so sure of yourself? Is it not more comely to be shy and self-conscious? This delicate question cannot be answered with a flat yes or no. We must take it apart.

First, self-consciousness. To be self-conscious is to be wondering how YOU look, what the audience is thinking of YOU, whether or not YOU are going to make a spectacle of YOURSELF. When you are self-conscious you are conscious of yourself. It is as simple as that. Self-consciousness is pride in a guise subtle enough to fool the most earnest of us.

Next, confidence. If you tackle the principles in this book and master them—given a chance to try them out and sand down your rough spots—of course you will have confidence. Confidence in your ability to be a good storyteller and speaker, and confidence in your ability (given a sporting chance) to hold an audience. And rightly so. This kind of confidence is merely the result of being well-versed in theory, well-disciplined by practice, and well-seasoned by experience. It is not only logical and right; it is essential. But how to reconcile it with . . .

Humility. Dr. Warren Filken of Northern Baptist Seminary in Chicago once said facetiously, "I was going to preach my sermon on 'Humility and how I attained it'—but there wasn't a big enough audience." That, spoken in jest, defines better than anything I've ever heard, what humility is not. This is no place for a learned discourse on humility; it is not the subject of this book, nor am I qualified. I only know—not from the erudite tomes of the sapients (and I've read volumes)—but from a firm conviction of the heart, that the relationship of humility to public speaking and the resultant lime-light is simply this: A talent for public speaking is a gift from God. To pretend it is not there is the height of ingratitude. Acknowledge it. Rejoice in it. Be glad you have it. The point is, don't ever forget that it is a gift from God. "Every good gift and every perfect gift is from above and cometh down from the Father . . ." (James 1:17) You may perfect it, but you did not create it in the first place, nor any of your other attributes that contribute to it. If you know this for a certainty, your attitude will be a combination of humbleness and gratitude, even though your presentation is exuding confidence. You can boom like a Boenerges, but somewhere down in your heart is that ever-present realization that left to yourself, you would cut a pretty small figure!

To sum up: The sum-total of "you" on the platform is made up of little things.

> Your dress
> Your grooming
> Your posture
> Your gestures
> Your poise

These things are interdependent; they affect each other adversely or to the good, depending on whether you neglect them or master them. Confidence and humility can be reconciled. Confidence is essential for a good presentation. Humility is remembering Who gave you the raw material to work out, so the good presentation is possible. Self-consciousness is a subtle form of pride. "That," as the efficiency experts say, "has got to go!"

Chapter 3

Your Voice

Well, what about it? Is it nasal? Harsh? Gutteral? Pitched too high? Do you find yourself with no voice at all—or worse still, with no breath at all, at the crucial moment?

Don't think too much about it. Without sincerity—without something to say, the most cultivated, the most golden voice will be as sounding brass and tinkling cymbals. If you really have something worthwhile to say and say it with all your heart, your audience will soon forget your voice.

But don't think too little of it, either. To just resign yourself to any shortcoming without a try, is to throw in the towel too easily. Remember the attention to small details; that is what success is made of. Many a story is spoiled by harsh or nasal tones of the speaker, or by being told in monotones. God gave you several strings in your voice-box. Play them all!

With a few simple tricks that you can practice at home, you can make your voice over—give it more power and resonance, lower its pitch. It is worth a try.

Briefly, a good voice depends on a *relaxed throat, deep breathing*, and *focused tone.*

Relaxed Throat

At first glance, your throat seems like a rather inaccessible part of your anatomy to control. But it can be controlled and there are three simple ways to do it.

1. Practice dropping your jaw. A loosened jaw is the key to success in voice-improvement. Drop it whenever you think of it, at odd moments, and only when you are alone. Dropping it in front of other people makes you look rather foolish. And unless they know you are practicing, it is very difficult to explain.

2. Practice yawning. Yawn also at odd moments, whenever you think of it. Yawn before you face your audience. Do not yawn while you are facing your audience. Unless they know you are practicing, this is also difficult to explain.

3. Practice humming. Humming is the basis of resonance. Hum up and down the scale. If you are tone-deaf, hum what you think might be up and down the scale. Then branch out into songs and hymns. It is not only good for your voice; it is good psychological therapy.

Deep Breathing

First you must know what it is not. It is not merely packing the lungs full of air. It is breathing from the diaphragm and sides of the trunk. Before beginning any exercises, place your hands on each side of the diaphragm. Imagine that there is a belt around that area, expanding and pushing against your hands. Then inhale and exhale through the mouth. The lower portions of the lungs should be filled first and emptied first, keeping the chest as quiet as possible. After you have mastered this, you may remove your hands from the sides of the diaphragm.

You will be needing them elsewhere. But do not forget to breathe as if they were still there.

1. Place your finger on the left nostril. Inhale through the right one, counting four—and hold, counting two.

Then place your finger on the right nostril and exhale slowly through the left one, counting four.

Leave your finger on the right nostril and inhale slowly through the left one, counting four. Hold it, counting two. Then place your finger on the left nostril and exhale slowly through the right one, counting four.

2. Flatten the tip of the nose and inhale through both nostrils, counting four and hold—counting two. Then exhale through the lips as if you were blowing out a candle, counting four.

Repeat these exercises, increasing your counts.

3. With the tongue lying flat, drop the jaw and yawn. Now close the lips and exhale through the nostrils, keeping the throat relaxed and open. This will give you a very peculiar expression and should be done in privacy.

4. With the throat relaxed and open, take a short quick breath through the mouth. Count two and exhale. Repeat, increasing the counts to the point where you become dizzy. At that point, it is a good idea to stop.

Focused Tones

To focus your tones, you merely bring them forward to the hard palate, to where the tip of your tongue rests when you say "L."

1. Inhale (and this always means with the throat open) and then exhale in a humming sound, thinking your tone against the hard palate.

2. Try it again, adding an "O" to the hum, thus:

        M-m-m-m-o

3. And again, adding "ah."

        M-m-m-m-o-ah

4. You are not finished yet. Add "m" again.

        M-m-m-m-o-ah-m

5. Now take "m" and add each vowel in turn.

        M-m-m-a-e-i-o-u (pronounced like

                double o, as in moon)

6. And just to relieve the monotony, use

        "N" instead of "M" and repeat.

        N-n-a-e-i-o-u

If you master these, you will never again try to "throw" your voice but will automatically focus your tones against the hard palate and project them by thinking them out and by breath control.

To sum up: A good voice depends on a relaxed throat, proper breathing and focused tone. You can improve your voice at home if you want to. Here is the know-how; the rest is up to you!

Chapter 4

Your Story

PREPARATION

The Bible Story

The easy way—and the lazy way—is to read it from a Bible story book. But the premise upon which all pedagogy is based is:

> You have to know a great deal
> in order to teach a little bit.

The result of knowing a great deal about your subject, whether or not you actually use it, is an aura of reserve power about you that people can sense. It is like listening to a great singer, not straining as he soars to the heights, but rather relaxing and enjoying it, knowing that he has even more power in reserve if he wants to use it.

I had a friend who was studying for her driver's test. She had studied long and hard, and when I asked her if she was ready for the fateful day, she said, "I'm so full of information, if you stuck me with a fork, it would ooze out like a roast." That is the way you should be—surfeited with every kind of information you can get hold of that pertains to your story.

Your Story

Arm yourself with:
 Your Bible
  A Bible dictionary
   A Bible handbook
    A Biblical geographical atlas
     Commentaries
      A Bible story book

First, read it from the Bible. Then read it again and again and AGAIN until you are so familiar with it there is not one part of it you cannot recall with ease. Then look up everything about it that you can find in your dictionary and handbook. Look up names, locations, battles, places, cities. If your story is about Noah—look up deluge, the ark and its construction and measurements. Find out what it was like, get familiar with it. If there are still points not clear to you, read any commentaries on the subject you can obtain. Don't depend too much on commentaries, however. Someone once said, "The Bible throws *so* much light on some of those commentaries!"

Now you may read the story in your Bible story book. You will read it much more intelligently—know much more about it. It will be real to you.

I wrote a radio script on Jonah once, for juniors. I read about whales for two weeks. It seemed to me that I found out everything about whales it was possible to know. I felt I could have gone on a whaling expedition and been quite intelligent about it by the time I got around to actually writing the script. But all that appeared in the final copy was:

> Boys and girls, I could tell you lots about whales. I could tell you about whales with small throats and sharp teeth that couldn't possibly swallow a man without tearing him to pieces. I could tell you about whales with big throats and bone plates instead of teeth, who could swallow a man. I

31

could tell you about the whaleshark of the Mediterranean, with a large throat and bone plates instead of teeth, that have swallowed men and animals and once even a reindeer! I could tell you about a little dog that was swallowed by a whale and rescued three days later and was still alive. I could tell you— but I won't. Because the Bible doesn't say anything about whales anyhow. It says "God prepared a great fish." And that's enough for me.

Even with all that information, one of my listeners challenged me with the fact that in Matthew, Christ Himself had said, "Jonah was three days in the belly of a whale." But I was able to answer that in the original the word had been "monster of the deep" and had been mistranslated "whale." That is what I mean by reserve power. You have to know a great deal to teach a little bit. You should be ready for anything.

Other Stories

The rules are pretty much the same as for Bible stories, only of course your sources of information are different. Get all the information you can, if it is non-fiction, and organize it.

THE KNOW-HOW OF ORGANIZING

In baking a cake, you simply read the recipe, get the called-for ingredients together, use them as directed, put the result in the oven, and you are reasonably certain that out will come a cake. It is relatively easy but even there, there's a catch. The ingredients *must be put together in a certain way*.

Your Story

So it is with a story, or, to be technical, composition. There are four things to remember.

Diction. When you organize your material for a story, you are putting together words, sentences, paragraphs. The way you put them together is called diction. As a story is no better than your arrangement, your choice of words, your expression of ideas—it is safe to say that the art of the storyteller has its roots in diction. But there is more to it than that.

Unity. The next step is getting things to be thought of together—*together.* Don't scatter your thoughts pell-mell throughout. Jot down everything you can think of to learn about your story. These are your ingredients. Then sort them out, use those ingredients where they belong. This is unity, But unity, like diction, may still not stick together properly. You must have . . .

Coherence, which is simply placing things in their proper order, an orderly progression to a climax—from the very beginning of a problem to its solution. You are journeying toward a destination. It should be a mountain-climbing journey with the peak at the end. If it is not strongest at the close, your story is badly arranged.

Transitions are the means by which you get from one point to the next. In reading, transitions are made by divisions into paragraphs and chapters. In radio, they are made by musical bridges. On the stage, they are made by curtains between the acts. But in storytelling, you make them yourself. By:
1. Narration
2. The pause

3. Change of pace
4. Change of style

If the various parts of your story are worked out in dialogue, your transitions are made by narration. If your entire story is straight narration to begin with, they are made by a pause before you go on to set the next "scene." If the next "scene" is a different mood, change your pace, change your style. The idea is to lure your audience into the next mood. You can never do this by rushing breathlessly from one scene to the next without "changing the scenery." You are either changing the mood, increasing or decreasing the excitement, or bridging time. If your listeners were reading the story, they would have a new paragraph or a new chapter to give them a warning that something new was in sight—so don't rush on. Give them a chance to catch up with you!

Now that you have diction, unity, coherence and transitions, the trick is to stop at the top! When the peak is reached, there is nowhere else to go. Don't add explanations, apologies, afterthoughts, provisos.

I remember a story of a man who was playing a lovely concerto. Things went well for awhile, then the thread of the melody began to repeat itself again and again. A gentleman in the wings gesticulated wildly and hissed— "Come off—come off—your time is up!"

And the pianist looked up frantically and hissed back— "I can't. I went past the ending!"

Just as you can get off the track in music and lose your ending—you can, unhappily, somehow lose your climax in the story and get hopelessly bogged down in afterthoughts. Don't go past the ending!

To put this all very simply, begin at the beginning,

keeping like things together, and proceed in an orderly progression toward the peak—and stop.

Now that you have read and read and READ—and have your wealth of information organized, here are three don'ts:

1. DON'T read it to your audience. Give them your attention.

2. DON'T memorize only the general ideas. Vital details can slip away when you are under the stress of facing your audience.

3. DON'T memorize verbatim. You will be wooden, chained to your material, restricted and inhibited. It is a phychological hazard—you are too easily thrown if you once forget something.

And two do's:

1. Write down the complete story with all the asides and all the extras and become so thoroughly familiar with it that it is a part of you.

2. Then don't just *tell* it, *live* it! You will find that the story will practically tell itself.

Prayer

In telling Bible stories, there is no other part of your preparation, however important, as vital as prayer. It is not just *any* story. You are dealing with the Word of God. You want it to be of the very highest quality, and He expects you to prepare—but don't leave Him out of it.

When Cornelius heard the wonderful story of salvation from Peter's lips, he was *already* ready to accept. Peter prayed—he was close to God.

When the jailor fell to his knees and cried, "What must I do to be saved?" his heart had already been prepared *before* Paul and Silas told him the story! They had been in the prison, praying.

When Rebecah gave just the right answer to Eliezer at the well, it was because Eliezer had been praying.

No matter how much information you have gathered or how thoroughly you have prepared—if, through your story, a person finds Christ, a life is rededicated, a problem is solved, it will be because you have prayed.

Christ said, "No man cometh unto the Father except I draw him." (Free translation) And He meant it.

Put your pupils' names on index cards, or on a list, and pray for them by name. Hold them up to God and ask Him to prepare their hearts.

If your audience is large, and index cards are out, then pray for them as a group—and pray for yourself. If you have prepared diligently, and prayed diligently, you can leave the rest to Him.

Chapter 5

The Introduction

The boys trooped in the church recreation room, bringing with them their flashlights, rubber bands for sling shots, the makings of spitballs and mittens wet from the snowball fight outside. When they took off their boots, "essence-of-sneakers" was added to the pungent aroma of wet mittens and other characteristic odors of boys—and the place took on the atmosphere of a gym locker room.

They tumbled into their seats, planned their strategy and prepared for their offensive. It might come during the singing. Or the story—if the story wasn't good.

The singing over, the teacher snatched a book of Bunyan's Holy War and held it high. She was not much bigger than the boys. They wondered if this one would be good.

"This is the most thrilling adventure story that has ever been written," she began. "It's a story of love and intrigue, of battles and armies—of helmets gleaming in the sun and banners waving in the breeze. It's a story of romance and blood and thunder! Listen. Once upon a time there was a great King whose name was Shaddai—and—"her voice lowered ominously, "a wicked giant named Diabolus. Now one day . . ."

The flashlights went out. The spitballs were crumpled into grubby fists. The slingshots were forgotten. And thirty boys sat on the edges of their seats—and listened.

This teacher knew how to start a story. And that is the point of this chapter. How to start. Because you can win them or lose them in the first two minutes!

Remember, your audience is not handed to you a ready-made unit. It is a miscellaneous collection of individuals, each one with a set of thoughts all his own.

Russ is wondering what to do about Sally, because Mary likes him now and Sally is Mary's best friend and they are both friends of Betty who liked him before Ann. Girls! Honestly. They could sure make life complicated. He looks at Biff and sighs . . . Biff looks at him without seeing.

Biff is there with his body but his mind is still back home defending himself against Alice who started a row that made them all late getting there. And all because he looked in her desk for something. Well it wasn't snooping. Couldn't a guy look in his sister's desk? Sisters! Honestly. He wonders what Pete does about his sister.

Peter has more important things on his mind than sisters. Dad wants to talk to him about something when they get back home. He takes mental inventory to see what he might have done. Can't think of a thing. He is roused from his reverie; somebody jerked his shoe-lace loose. Oh. Dave the runt. Peter cuffs him in mock rage.

Dave ducks and reaches for the other shoe-lace. Why is it that all the other guys suddenly started to grow and he didn't. He is the same age. Anyhow, everybody has to admit he is a live-wire. Not like ole Ed here. Why ole Ed . . .

Yes, for every one in your audience, there is a separate set of thoughts, important and unimportant, competing against you. At the sound of your voice they come to attention, but the mere sound of your voice will not hold them any longer than a few seconds. After that, you are on your own. If your introduction isn't interesting, they will go back to wool-gathering again.

It would hardly be fair to say that one part of the story is more important than any other part. It is ALL imporant and it must all be good. But it is certainly a fact that the introduction is the best place to win them—and the worst place to lose them! It is easier to win them at once than to get them back after you have lost them in the beginning. *You will win or lose in the first three minutes, depending on how you begin.*

The introduction should be like the gun that signals the start of a game or a race. Get ready—get set—GO!

It should be a promise of exciting things to come. Actually, it is bait to get attention in such a way that it will be kept.

The function of an introduction is to get started. It is a means to an end, not an end in itself. Think of it as an entry-way. An entry-way is merely a means to get into the house. No matter how intriguing it is, it is not the main attraction; it is never bigger or more important than the house itself. Just as an entry-way never obscures the house —a good introduction is never so long or so important that it obscures the story. The porch is the way in, the house is the thing!

Various types of introductions serve various purposes. Do you want to, by inuendo, explain or clarify the point to the story? Is your story a part of a serial? Do you simply want to capture interest? Or are you at a loss as to how to start at all? Choose your introduction to suit your purpose. They are not all alike, nor do they accomplish the same thing. It depends on your story. Here are some basic types; you can custom-make them to accomplish your goal.

Storytelling—It's Easy!

To explain the point of the story. In the story of Jonah, if you simply say, "Now boys and girls, we are going to have the story of Jonah" you are off to a bad start. Try this:

> Would you like to hear the story of Jonah? Well, once upon a—(*pause. Look them over. You won't find one eager face*). I know just how you feel. I can see the wheels in your heads going around. You're thinking—"I know that one. I know it backwards. I could start in the middle and tell it toward both ends with my hands tied behind my back."
>
> I know how you feel. Everyone thinks he knows the story of Jonah. Why, just a few years ago, if one of my own children had asked me to tell him the story of Jonah, it might have gone something like this:
>
> (*Pretend you are knitting*) "Jonah? Why of course—everyone knows the story of Jonah. Knit two, purl two, knit two together and proceed as in row four. What on earth did I do in row four? Oh. Well, Jonah. Well. Jonah was a man who —was in the water. And he . . . I don't know how he got there. Anyhow, there he was—swimming about, and along came a big fish—and swallowed him. And he was—why did the fish swallow him? I don't know. Anyhow, there he was. And he stayed in the fish three days and three nights and then the fish threw . . . sp . . . tossed . . . him up—on the shores of . . . (*pause*). Well, anyhow, he picked himself up and went to—(*pause*). I don't know where he went. I don't think I know where he came from. (*pause*) I declare, there MUST be more of a point to the story of Jonah than that or it wouldn't be in the Bible."
>
> (*Look at them over your knitting. They will be delighted. You have taken them into your confidence. You have also flattered them, for you are assuming that they know there is a point to the story of Jonah. They probably don't but now they are anxious to!*)
>
> OF COURSE there's a point to the story of Jonah. (*Now You Are Serious*) Why Jonah is one of the most thrilling missionary stories written. It's a story about a man who ran away from God. Listen. Once upon a time God put His hand on a man for a great mission—and that man's name was Jonah. Now one day, God said to Jonah . . .

The Introduction

You have accomplished two things. You have already established the point of your story, which is the fact that there is more of a point to the story of Jonah than most people realize, and you have challenged them to listen to a story they might otherwise feel they already know too well. It is kept from being irreverent by making it plain that that is not the way the story should to be told—it is simply the way you would have told it—before you knew better!

There are many stories that can have introductions to explain their points. The point to the story of Abraham can be explained by a discourse on knitting mittens—a step at a time, simply trusting to the step-by-step instructions to see that they don't come out all thumbs. Abraham's life was like that; he followed instructions.

The point to the story of Noah can be explained by a discourse on model airplanes and how those mysterious patterns in the kit—"Match AA to ZZ and glue on notches indicated . . ." do finally make an airplane. Noah is a pattern story. A picture of something to come. A type of Christ.

There is no end of interesting introductions that will clarify your story-point. Custom-make your own!

To start a new chapter in a serial. Recapitulation is, of course, a must. It can be very dull or very interest-catching. Just don't ramble into practically telling last week's story over again. Organize your introduction to get off to a good start.

> *When king Astyages gave his baby grandson to his general Harpagus to be killed, he thought that was the end of it. (Lower your voice to confidential low tones) But we know

---

*From Herodotus' account of Cyrus.

41

that Harpagus gave that baby to a goatherd. And we know the goatherd took it home to his wife. And we know they swapped it for their own baby who had died that very day, and kept the live baby for themselves. And we know that Astyages' grandson is living in the goatherd's cottage, learning to creep, learning to walk, learning to play soldiers—growing up. Astyages thinks he is dead. But we know differently. And there's trouble ahead! Now—on with the story!

The children who were there last week have their memories refreshed in a streamlined account. The ones who weren't there have enough to get them started—and interested. Don't ramble!

To simply capture interest. Instead of saying, "This is a story of Joshua's long day and the battle between the Israelites and the kings of Canaan . . ." try this:

Did you ever hear of the League of nations? Did you think it was something new? Did you ever hear of a league of nations that was started 3200 years ago? Do you like stories that begin with "Once upon a time there was a king? A wicked king?" Well, this is a story about a wicked king. He even had a horrible name. Adonizedec.

Now one morning, a humble servant tiptoed along an upper corridor in this king's palace, stopped by a huge carved door—and knocked. (*knock*) No answer. So he pushed the door open and the guards were asleep and the king was asleep and this fellow had to wake them all up so the biggest event in history could get started.

This king *had* to get up. He was the one who started this league of nations—all the kings in the land of Canaan. They'd banded together because of a general called Joshua and the Israelites, who were sweeping into the land of Canaan, mowing down everything before them—who were reputed to have a living God!

He nibbled his royal breakfast from his royal tray, got into his royal clothes, brushed his royal beard—and at last he was ready.

The Introduction

An hour later in one of the downstairs rooms of the palace all the bigwigs of Canaan sat around a highly polished mahogany table. Their faces were reflected double in the table, which was dreadful, for they were quite bad enough to begin with. Adonizedic was speaking. As he spoke, he looked grim. And they listened hard. There was TROUBLE ahead!

You can take almost any story and set an imaginary scene to start off in a way to promise excitement and interest. Here is one, for instance, that is quite ordinary; in fact it is not even an adventure story. You COULD say that there was a lady named Miss Jackson, who visted the hospital every day. But how much more fun to say (*with a lilt in your voice*):

Miss Jackson went into the front door of the hospital, nodded to the people at the reception desk and said, "Hi!" and sailed across the big lobby. She went to the elevator and the elevator man said "Hi!" He didn't ask her where she was going. He knew . . . they all knew. They'd been expecting her. He let her off at four, and she automatically turned to the right. She'd been there many times. It was the children's ward.

Nothing very exciting or adventurous in that beginning. But you have at least set a scene, promised something *alive*, introduced some people.

Let your audience know you are going some place. Whether it is a story of an exciting battle . . .

All night long the great army marched across the plains of Canaan. All night long, the people inside the walls of the city barricaded their gates and got ready for the onslaught. All night long they marched and watched—and waited. For in the morning one of the most exciting battles in history was about to take place. And this is how it began. Listen. Once upon a time there was a king who . . .

Or the story of an obscure man . . .

> This is the story of an ordinary man who might have lived and died and never been heard of again except that one day something happened to him that changed his life—and affected the destiny of nations. It started this way . . .

Or simply a mother hen hatching out a couple of duck eggs . . .

> There in the corner of the barnyard, mother Fluffruffle sat on her nest clucking over her eggs. She *knew* the eggs were going to hatch—but what she *didn't* know . . . well, she was in for the surprise of her life!

Something is about to happen, and it is very interesting. Make it interesting! It's an attitude on your part, and you can transmit it to them whether it's an exciting story or a quiet one.

Arouse their curiosity. You could wrap up a whole plot with, "This is a story of a prophet who told king Ahab it would not rain and then hid in the wilderness while his prophecy came true." But why give it all away? How much better to say:

> Nobody could stop him. He dashed into the courtyard, past the guards, up the steps, and into the throne room—right up to the king himself. "As the Lord Liveth," he cried—"there shall not be dew nor rain these many days except according to my word."
> The king cried out for the guards to stop him, but he turned on his heel and disappeared into the crowd!

Then you can begin at the beginning. They'll let you. You have their undivided attention. Go back and fill in the facts. Your introduction says, "Who was this prophet?

The Introduction

Who was the king? What's going to happen?" Give them just enough in the beginning to pique their curiosity and fill them in later!

Give it a surprise twist. Try approaching your story from a different angle than the ordinary. Is your story about Hezekiah? Instead of starting with "Once there was a king who . . ." start with:

> Once upon a time there was a sundial right in the middle of a palace courtyard. The sun cast its shadow from a tall obelisk on a huge flight of steps, and told the time. Beyond the sundial were palace gardens, and beyond the gardens was the palace. On the day our story opens—the palace was hushed—the curtains were drawn. Inside, a great king was dying. And this sundial was about to play a vital part in his destiny . . .

Is your story about the boy's lunch that fed five thousand? Instead of starting with the *boy*—start with the *day*.

> The day started out like any ordinary day. The boy's mother packed him a lunch and he started out toward the lake never dreaming that this was going to be one of the most exciting days in his life!

A brief dramatization. Choose a dramatic portion of the story and plunge into it at once.

> *Mr. Carnal Security: "Mr. Godly Fear, are you not well? Here is a cordial of Mr. For-get-Good's making—delightful. One sip of this and you will—eh, get into the spirit of things."
> Mr. Godly-Fear: "I do not care for your cordial."
> Mr. Carnal-Security: "Come, come. It'll take the weight off your mind."
> Mr. Godly Fear: "I do have something on my mind. I would like to speak to these people. (*He shouts to the others*) You elders, chiefs, natives of Mansoul."

---

*From Bunyan's Holy War.

45

Mr. Carnal Security: "Mr. Godly Fear, you really look ill. If you want to retire . . ."

Mr. Godly Fear: "No, I don't want to retire. You have stripped Mansoul of her strength."

Mr. Carnal Security: "I've done nothing of the sort. What is the matter with you? Why are you so timid? I'm on your side, only you're for doubting and I'm for being confident."

Mr. Godly Fear: "Confident of what?"

Mr. Carnal Security: "Mansoul is impregnable!"

Mr. Godly Fear: "Mansoul *was* impregnable, with a proviso—complete dependence on Emanuel."

Mr. Carnal Security: "But . . ."

Mr. Godly Fear: "No, don't interrupt me. I will not be silent. (*He shouts to the others*) Do you question that your strength is gone? I'll answer your question WITH a question; Where IS Prince Emanuel?"

(*To Your Audience*) This scene took place in a huge banquet hall. But the story really began months before that. Once upon a time . . .

This type of introduction can be fascinating. But reserve it until you have studied—and practiced the chapter on dialogue!

Something different. This is something you might try occasionally before class-proper even begins, but do not try it too often!

* (*In Mysterious Tones*) The general stood over the table, intent on what he was doing. He had a rabbit strapped to the board, and he was busy slitting the loose skin on its abdomen (or tummy if the children are young). He took a note, put it inside, carefully sewed up the slit—and finally when it was done, he handed the rabbit to a servant who was standing near by. "Deliver this to Cyrus," he said. "If you do not deliver it to Cyrus personally, I'll kill you."

---

*From Herodotus' account of Cyrus.

And stop there. Take the attendance. Have the preliminaries. Take the offering. You'll get their carfare home in the offering—they are so interested they are hypnotized.

This is obviously not an introduction you should get in the habit of using. But if you are desperate for a new way to get their interest, it is certainly novel. Tuck it away for an emergency!

To sum up, introductions may be:
1. To explain the point of the story.
2. To start a new chapter in a serial.
3. To merely capture interest (Let your audience know you are going someplace, arouse their curiosity, give it a surprise twist).
4. A brief dramatization of an exciting portion of the story.
5. A sample, before the preliminaries.

But no matter which kind you use, it.must be an attention-getter, the bait, the signal to start. If you follow these simple rules, your introductions will always be a promise of better things to come. Your listeners have been brought to attention by the sound of your voice, but it takes that promise to hold them there!

Remember, your audience is not handed to you a ready-made unit. It is a miscellaneous collection of individuals, each one with a set of thoughts all his own. Your job is to make them one unit—concentrated on one idea—your story. You have a better chance if you begin right. It is easier to win them at once than to lose them and try to win them back.

The introduction's the thing! And there is an introduction custom-made for every story, if you look for it.

Chapter 6

The Application In The
Bible Story

In a large Sunday school in the midwest, a teacher asked her wee pupils to draw their conception of the flight into Egypt. One drawing turned in was of an airplane with a figure in front and three in the back. "It's Joseph and the baby Jesus and His mother Mary," the little one explained.

"And who's that in front?" the teacher wanted to know.

"That's Pontious—the pilot."

Obviously, somewhere along the line, somebody had missed the point.

In plays of bygone days the audience always got the point of the story. The author stepped outside the curtain and delivered the epilogue, which was a careful explanation of just what he was attempting to get across. He took no chances. *And nobody was left in doubt.*

In court, the jury always gets the point of the trial, pro and con. The lawyers step up to the jury-box and deliver their summations of just what they're attempting to get across. They take no chances. *Nobody is left in doubt.*

So it is in storytelling, your listeners should always get the point of the story. You step out from behind the story and deliver your explanation of just what you were attempting to get across.

Don't take for granted that they got the point. A pastor friend of mine from Brooklyn walked past a class of little boys who were repeating the Lord's Prayer. He quietly removed one and took him to his study for a chat. The little fellow obviously needed straightening out. He had been saying, "Lead us not into Penn Station."

The first rule of application is—don't omit it! You must do what the bygone authors did and what the lawyers do today. But here the similarity ends. What you *do* is the same—but how you *do* it is different. You must do it more subtly, or they will slip away like quick-silver. Tie up the ends, wind it up, clear up the point, but be sure to:

Make it as real as the story. Don't finish the story, draw a mental curtain, pause, and then in a let-down voice, give your application in a dreary summation. Leap into it with the same intensity as the story. It is real! It is vital! It is something exciting and tremendous that we should know.

If your listeners are children, pick one point and drive it home quickly, as if it were the most exciting news in the world.

Apply it to them personally. If it is at all possible, give it a personal up-to-date twist. Your listeners are interested in themselves. Turn their thinking to themselves at once.

After Cyrus the Mede had cut his niche, made his conquests, gained his spoils—we find that his life had already been written in the ancient Jewish scrolls. *"I have known thee, Cyrus, I have called thee by name, before

---
*Isaiah:45

49

thou were born." At the end of this glorious climax, how thrilling to suddenly bring it up to date, make it personal.

> God knew you. Before you were born. He knew what your name would be. He called you by your name before you even got here! He has planned your life, fought your battles, knows every problem you will face. This is the most important fact in life for you to know. To go one step in life without Him is foolish—when He knows more about you than you do yourself!

After the story of Hezekiah, how real it becomes if you turn to your listeners with:

> Put an ad in the paper and sell your things. Straighten out your room. Say goodbye to your friends. You are going to die next Tuesday. That's a startling thought, isn't it? It's one thing to talk about God in an abstract way and another thing to face the fact that you might see Him next Tuesday.

If there is any possible way you can do it, bring it down to everyday living and present your listener with a challenge for himself, or a personal decision to make, or a personal question to answer. Don't let him go away with "that was a swell story!" But rather, "What am I going to do about this?"

Keep it simple. Remember, one point, successfully brought home is better than a dozen points that drop on indifferent ground. It is a temptation to tell them all you know, every facet, every shade, of the many truths in the Word of God. But in doing this you run the risk of giving them more than they can absorb and in the end, you've driven no point home at all. Choose the point you wish to make and drive it home briefly, concisely, personally.

After the application, stop! After you've made your point

don't add provisos, afterthoughts, further explanations, anti-climaxes, that weaken and detract. Don't suddenly remember some detail you'd left out and attempt to put it in. You've followed the rules and your application has been strong and successful. Now don't, in the name of good storytelling, undo it!

You may prefer to weave it throughout the story. Pick out a point you want most to get across—and it is best with children to make it one point—and peck away at it. In this way you are getting your application across by the "drip" method. A drip at a time.

Actually it does not matter whether the application is woven throughout or placed at the end. It will be accepted or rejected not on the basis of where you put it, but on the basis of how you present it.

Your application is the test of your own relationship with God. The Rules we have set down are to give you practical help, but they can do no more than that. The application is a spiritual matter, the portion of the story when the light of God shines through. Methods are only a "help." Your relationship with God is the real measure of the success of your application.

Remember—the application is a must. It is the real test of the story itself. It reveals how much "meat" and how much "dessert" was there all the time. It gives them something to take home with them.

The purpose of many stories is to arouse the listener to action. The purpose of Bible stories is to point the listener to God, to help him in his Christian growth, to challenge him, to bring him to a decision. The purpose of any good story is to at least make a point!

And like the author, like the lawyer—you must take no chances. Nobody should be left in doubt.

Chapter 7

Delivery

This, you say, is where you bog down hopelessly. A story you can read, even the extras you can gather together, your facts you can organize—but the intricacies and mysteries of proper delivery! That is too much. Leave it to the experts!

Nonsense. It is simple when you know what it is all about.

When sons number one and two were small, they came home from school one day, around the driveway and into the kitchen like a couple of bicycle sirens.

"We're not going to school tomorrow!" they shrieked, and deposited on the table two mysterious pink slips of paper. "You have to sign them. They're permission to stick us with a needle!"

"Why, it's nothing," I said calmly, glancing at the offending slips.

"Nothing!" they wailed. "The needle is a foot big and they stick it right in you and people faint and everything! It's a 'Schick' test!"

They had me there. The very phonetics of the word "Schick" are ominous. If only somebody named Brahms had invented it! I picked up the slips, and my offspring looked at me as if they were death warrants.

Then I had an idea.

"How would you like to be the bravest boys in school

tomorrow?" I asked, as I got a small syringe and a skin needle and popped them into a pan to boil. "How would you like to know all about what that silly little Schick test is—when none of the other kids do?"

They stared at me with suspicion. I got the rest of my ingredients ready, the cotton, the alcohol, a clean towel.

"Now," I said matter-of-factly in my deep professional voice. "I am the doctor. And you are the bravest boys in the school. The line has formed. And everybody is fainting and everything. All but you. Stick out your arm."

Son number one did so with grave misgivings. Son number two watched from a safer vantage point, wedged in between the refrigerator and the wall.

"And what is your name, my good man?" I said in my best doctor's voice. "You seem to be the bravest boy in this school."

He did not answer. He was speechless with fright.

"All those other children are fainting and everything. They seem to think that this is something mysterious and frightening," I told him, man to man. "But we know that it is just a little—tiny—prick! There."

I waited. He looked at his arm incredulously. Then at me.

"Is that all?" he squeaked. "Did you do it?"

"It's done."

"With that little tiny needle?"

"With that little tiny needle."

"Is that all it'll be tomorrow?"

"That's all. Just a tiny prick, under your top skin."

Son number two came out from his hiding. "Is that all the bigger the needle is?" His voice went up out of range, soundless. And he thrust out his arm. Then we all laughed. I signed the slips with a flourish. And we laughed again.

Next day I waited for them to come around the driveway again, like triumphant warriors, to announce that they were indeed the bravest boys in the school. They did.

They had been frightened by the unknown. As soon as the mystery cleared and they saw how simple it was, they went forth to conquer like a couple of seasoned veterans.

The art of delivery doesn't sound as ominous as "Schick" to be sure, but it is hidden behind so much jargon that most of us do not have the courage to even begin. We leave that to the professionals. Let us dig up the bug-aboo and expose it for what it is—a chimera. Proper delivery is a know-how that is fun to discover, easy to master, and valuable-beyond-belief to possess!

General Points on Delivery

Salesmanship I dashed into a huge department store in Providence one afternoon—into the housewares and up to the pressure-cookers. I had a radio program in another hour and was not disposed to linger. I also had an account there, which is always dangerous. You are apt not to stop to haggle over prices.

"I want a pressure-cooker," I said breathlessly to a startled salesgirl. "I'm in a hurry, just wrap me up one. Any one will do."

She recovered promptly. She was not going to be done out of her sales-pitch. "This one," she said, fondling it lovingly, "is wonderful. It is simple, needs no watching . . ." But my eye had traveled to another one that had so many gadgets and so much trim it looked like a space ship.

"THIS one," I said. "How does it work?"

Her smile stiffened. "Of course you have to watch the pressure on that one," she said, and began to turn dials, un-screw, manipulate mysterious gadgets. "You adjust this—

and turn this. And fasten this. And you have to watch your pressure. When it's done, it turns off automatically and . . ."

She suddenly bent over, put her head down on her arm, and delivered a blow on the counter with her fist. "The cover collapses and the whole mess falls in your food. I CAN'T sell these pressure cookers—I just don't like them!"

I had the sudden impulse to offer her my hanky and say "blow." I did the next best thing. "Wrap me up the one you like," I said gently. "It must be terrific."

"Oh, it is." She wrapped it gleefully, chattering about its good points. I went home firmly convinced that I had met the funniest, the most engaging salesman on record. And that I had bought absolutely the best pressure cooker in Rhode Island.

Why?

I believed in it because SHE believed in it. She had sold me utterly because she was sold herself.

If you are not absolutely sold on your story, you cannot sell it to others. The I-don't-care attitude gets an I-don't-care response. Your listeners will be sold according to the degree you are sold. If your whole attitude says, "this is an amazing story! It's so good I can hardly wait to tell it!"—then they can hardly wait to hear it. You must be a good salesman.

Sincerity explains itself. It means without veneer, without shellac. The real thing. You cannot affect sincere delivery. It is an attitude. You have to honestly feel that way. Say what you believe—believe what you say—without affectation. Speak with excitement because you are excited, with sadness because you are sad, with happiness because you are happy. If you are not sincere, you won't fool anyone, especially children. If you are sincere, you won't have to!

Earnestness is a most important word for you to consider, especially when your material deals with the Word of God. It means "to be bowed down with the solemness of your message." It is important, and for this reason.

In our desire to compete with the excitement of this wonderful world, we are apt to go overboard and dress up our Bible stories until they are out-of-bounds—and with the best intentions, we can be flippant with the Word of God. The great doctrines of the Bible are solemn things indeed.

How to avoid being flippant with them?

There are no rules. It is basically an attitude. If you are serious and worshipful about the things of God, you can be gay, you can be humorous, you can be imaginative —and you will never go beyond the realm of good taste. The Holy Spirit Himself will check you. Somehow you will know how far you can go. Never be flippant with the Word of God. Be earnest.

Wholeheartedness. Back in the days before tape-recorders, on which you can wipe out your mistakes and splice together only the successful tries, we were cutting a record one day that was to be entered in a national radio contest. Everyone was tense as the needle was put down on the master record on which there was no such reprieve. We had rehearsed for hours; everyone was tired. The orchestra was ready. The sound effects man was at a table just out of my reach with, among other things, a crumpled piece of cellophane, for on page six we had a fire. The red light went on. The director pointed. We were off!

All went well until the bottom of page five. I read the lines with tense excitement. "The walls—the walls—the very earth seemed to rent and give way beneath them."

And then, from the periphery of my vision, I saw something that froze me to a point. My sound effects man had fallen asleep. He had stiffened out like a pole and slid partly under the table, only his elbows keeping him from disappearing from sight.

I tried to reach him with my foot. Frontways. Sideways. To no avail. He was a foot beyond my touch. I glanced frantically at people posted with various duties about the studio. They looked back helplessly. Either nobody could leave his post—or was frozen stiff with fear. I had no lines with which to fade off my mike. All, apparently, was lost.

The top of page six came with the certainty of death itself and for a moment seemed like it. My lines were, "Through the smoke and soot the cry went up . . . Fire!" It was supposed to be delivered in a subdued dramatic whisper.

"Through the smoke and dust the cry went up . . . Fire!" It was a moment of decision.

I dashed over to his table and cried into his ear and his mike . . . "FIRE!!!"

He came up glazed and shaken, beating the air, crumpling his wad of cellophane. We had our fire, and the record proceeded—with some difficulty, for everyone had gone into spasms of silent laughter—the only kind you can indulge in, in a studio when the red light is on.

But that record won the first national prize!

I can see how it happened. I can see the judges as they listened, with their little "ummms" and "Uhhums" of approval and disapproval. Then when they got to the part where I shouted so desperately, I can hear them say, "That's IT. That's the ONE. Why that woman shouted fire as if she were ON fire! What wholeheartedness!"

It was, if nothing else, wholehearted. And wholeheartedness won the prize.

Tell your story with wholeheartedness. Give it all you have. If it is worth telling at all, it is worth telling with all your heart.

Enthusiasm is a trait that is so powerful that it can be downright dangerous if used wrongly. It excites enthusiasm in others, rouses them to respond. It is the spark-plug that sets off dormant action.

When Cyrus the Mede wanted to raise an army, Herodotus tells us that he called thousands upon thousands of men to a place that was like a natural amphitheatre—mountains on each side of a valley with a natural rock platform at the end. And when they got there, their orders were to pull scrub-brush on the mountains.

They complied grumpily, thinking they would at least get lunch.

But lunch time came—and no lunch. They pulled all afternoon, thinking desperately—at least—dinner! But no dinner either. They dropped in their tracks, exhausted, decided to rest and go home at dawn.

But when the sun came up, there in the valley were oxen and goats and sheep roasting on spits. The aroma was irresistible. Before you could say "pass the butter," Cyrus had all that delicious food passed among the men. After they had eaten, he made the speech that sparked them into action. Response he desired—response he got.

> "Do you want to spend the rest of your lives like yesterday," he shouted from the platform—"your bellies empty and no spoils for reward?"
>
> They certainly did not.
>
> "Or," he cried, "Will you spend your lives with me as your leader—your bellies full—and spoils for reward like today—a life of adventure!"
>
> Their voices rent the air. Legs o' lamb were thrown up in the air like hats in a baseball arena.

They certainly did.

And they did! He sparked enough enthusiasm in them to practically conquer the world. They even got into the un-get-in-able Babylon just in time to send the Jews back to Jerusalem to build up the Temple, which of course was what God intended all the time. But He used Cyrus' enthusiasm to do it!

Enthusiasm is dynamite. It is one of the most powerful weapons a speaker can have. It got an army to follow Cyrus. It will get an audience to follow you. It is not a device, a trick, an affectation. It is an attitude.

What are you like when you are enthusiastic? If you are the quiet type naturally, let this be a comfort to you. Enthusiasm does not necessarily mean a lot of noise! I had a class of Junior boys once, around a huge table and behind a screen. On the other side of that screen were other people. Noise was out. Enthusiasm, however, was not. In low tones we went, tale by tale, down through the corridors of history, fighting, conquering, learning, daring, peering through the dust of battle to see how it came out. The tones were low, but they shot sparks of enthusiasm into the air as we warmed to our subject. In the midst of one close battle, a boy thrust his leg out behind him to change his position, and knocked over the screen. He got down quickly, put the screen aright, scrambled back to his position, without missing a beat. Not another head was turned in his direction. They were too interested in the story. Enthusiasm had glued them to the spot.

You can hiss, roar, fight battles, march and shout—all in a whisper, if the enthusiasm is there. Enthusiasm is an attitude in you that will spark enthusiasm in others—demand a response, get action. Noisy or quiet, it is a weapon to reckon with.

Animation does not mean that you must jump about like a monkey on a stick. You can be animated standing or sitting still. With your eyes. With your facial expressions. With your gestures. With your whole being. It is cause and effect—the natural result of wholeheartedness and enthusiasm and being completely sold on your subject.

A broken heart. When Jenny Lind came to America, she had every audience at her feet. A critic wrote of her, "She is wonderful beyond belief. Now if she would only get her heart broken, she would be great." His words were prophetic. He married her—and broke her heart. After that, audiences were at her feet with acclaim. She made them weep. A new quality had been added—a new power. She was able to wring tears from others; she was intimately acquainted with suffering herself. And somehow they knew. Suffering cries out to suffering—there is a mystical rapport.

You do not have to marry a critic or otherwise have your heart broken in order to tell a good story, of course. But it is true, that in serious storytelling, you cannot wring a response to pathos unless you are acquainted with it yourself, either empirically or by empathy. If you are not out for serious storytelling but are merely interested in telling Bible stories to children, a different aspect of the same rule applies. A broken heart does not necessarily mean tragedy. If you have a deep personal love for God, a worshipful attitude toward Him, an immense gratitude for what He has done, your delivery will have the same power to wring a response. Moody had a happy marriage and as far as we know, no great tragedy touched his life, but he could never read the Scriptures without weeping!

Be Yourself. This seems like a paradox, but it is possible to learn all the techniques of dramatics and still not be "arty" about it. If you absorb them until they are actually a part of you—the result will be complete naturalness. The highest form of art is to banish every obvious trace of it. Be yourself!

To sum up: The general requisites of good delivery are:
1. Salesmanship
2. Sincerity
3. Earnestness
4. Wholeheartedness
5. Enthusiasm
6. Animation
7. A broken heart
8. Be Yourself!

They cannot be affected. They are basically attitudes.

THE FINER POINTS OF DELIVERY

Emphasis

A good decorator knows the importance of emphasis. He calls it a focal point. The eye is drawn to the fireplace, a picture, some important aspect of the room. Everything else is subordinate. A good dress designer knows the same secret. The eye is directed to a bow, an accent, a sweep of material, a focal point. Everything else is subordinate. This rule gives the room, the dress a distinction. It makes everything else fall into proper place; you remember what the decorator and the designer want you to remember.

In good delivery, this is done by emphasis, only there is not one focal point; invariably there are many. They must stand out; you must manipulate your listeners so they will remember what you want them to remember. This can be done by:

Strong words or phrases. They do not have to be sixty-nine dollar words, or powerful words, though they can be if your story is directed to older children or adults. They can be very simple for children. The point is, they are given more importance than anything else in that particular sequence.

In the story of creation, after the trees and the birds and the beasts and the fish and all the rest are described:

> And when God finished the world,
> He looked at it—and it was *just right.*

God made no mistakes; that is what you want them to remember.

Lowering or raising the voice: Raising the voice for emphasis is just "doing what comes naturally"—we need no prodding to do that. But did you ever think of lowering your voice for emphasis? Try it occasionally. You will be delighted with the results. It sometimes has a more dramatic and ·startling effect than a shout. In the story of Joshua, I was telling a group of Junior boys about the alliance of the Israelites and the Hivites—and how the Israelites had been tricked into it because they had acted on impulse.

> "You—you Hivites of Gibeon," shouted the Israelites. "For that you will be our slaves forever!"
> Well, that was alright with the Hivites. It was better to be live slaves than dead enemies. Their trick had worked. It was the greatest hoax in history. The whole nation of Israel

had been fooled by a few old men! And do you know why?
Because when they were making their plans . . . (I lowered
my voice to a whisper and in evenly spaced words, said:)
They—forgot—to—ask—God.

After the story, a boy was overheard informing his
father of an earth-shaking fact. "And do you know why?"
he demanded. Then he lowered his voice to an ominous
whisper and delivered the punch. "They—forgot—to—
ask—God!"
He remembered what I wanted him to remember.

Pausing briefly after important point. If you make your
point and then rush on, you are apt to undo what you've
just accomplished. A slight pause after something important is a subtle form of emphasis.

Repetition. If there is one central point you wish to em-
phasize, sprinkle it throughout the story. Take the account
of an old man who faced what seemed like insurmountable
difficulties and overcame them. The story is a succession
of these difficulties, a succession of climaxes. But the point
of emphasis is always the same:

At the end of his first triumph—

And an ordinary old man prayed an ordinary prayer—and
God answered.

And as he succeeds against odds again:

So an ordinary man prayed an ordinary prayer—and God
answered.

And finally, as his triumph is complete over his antago-
nists:

Because an ordinary man prayed an ordinary prayer—and God answered.

Repetition of one central point, strategically spaced throughout the story, is one of the best forms of emphasis.

Echo repetition. This is either repeating the word or phrase several times:

> Don't go with the crowd. *That was the crowd* that stood on the hillside, *that was the crowd* that laughed, *that was the crowd* that didn't believe—*that was the crowd* that was—lost.

Or casting thoughts in the same mold:

> She shouted at him, she phoned him, she wrote him, she followed him home, she was kind to him, she was mean to him, she threatened him, she plagued him—but to no avail. Johnny wouldn't give up the coveted tadpole.

This kind of repetition has the effect of an echo. It sticks in the mind!

Proportion. If your emphasis is not on finer points, but one general thought in the story, the rule is to dwell longest on what is most important. Don't overshadow it by too high a ratio of incidentals.

VARIETY

Why is it—when you've been resting long enough, you want to be up and doing. Or when you've been up and doing awhile, you want to rest? Or if you've been munching sweets all day, nothing appeals to you like a ham on rye. Or if you've been listening to a speaker drone on and on in a monotonous sameness for too long, you wish you could unscrew your arms and legs and change them around just to relieve the monotony. If only he would shout, change his tone or position, or even burst into song! Anything for a change.

Variety, as the sages say, is the spice of life. It can also be the magic ingredient in your delivery that makes you fascinating to listen to, and increase both the attendance and the attention of your audiences. You can get it in your delivery by mastering a few simple tricks.

Pacing

A story can be told without color or interest—without scenes or moods or various pitches of excitement, without even a climax. The teller might just as well have begun in the middle and told it toward both ends. The same story could be told with scenes, moods, increasing tension and a well-defined climax. The difference is often merely pacing.

What you can do with pacing is sheer magic. You can create moods, fight battles, march armies, regulate and change the speed of action and literally manipulate your listeners out of one mood and into the next.

Pace to a standstill. Do you want to slow down the action? Do it by pacing. Like this:

> (*Very Fast*) The lightning flashed and the thunder crashed— and mother Fluffruffle cried—"Wuuuk puk puk puk puk PUK" and called her chicks and they came running. She lifted her wings and under they went—squiggling, squirming, stepping on each others' heads (*Slower*) And she settled her wings back over them and little feet stuck out underneath (*Slower*) and

she sang to them till the storm was over. Then she stuck her head in her fluffy neck feathers and sighed. And the moonlight spread—like a bucket of paint—(*Slower*) spilling and spreading over the barnyard (*Slower*) over the meadow—down to the pond. And finally (*Slower*) everybody—in the barnyard—was asleep.

One danger here is that you could put your listeners to sleep. Don't overdo it!

Pace to a climax. Want to speed up the action? Like this:

(*Start Out Slowly*) All evening long, the soldiers watched by the gates of Babylon—watched the mighty Euphrates river flowing through the gates, watched the water, waited for it to go down. At first it went down imperceptibly—and then (*Faster*) more noticeably. They watched and waited. (*Faster*) Now it was faster—(*Faster*) they tensed themselves for action (*Faster*)—faster. They watched the gates, the water mark on them getting lower and lower until (*Faster*) they could see the bottom of the gates—and the water went down and down (*Faster*) and at last the cry went through the night—"Under the gates! March under the gates! Under the gates of Babylon!"

To do this successfully, you must be speaking slowly to begin with. If you are already speaking rapidly, there won't be any place to go.

And remember, in speeding up or slowing down—do it imperceptibly, don't suddenly increase or decrease speed as if you had pressed a button and shifted into another gear.

Pacing for rhythm. Want to march an army across the pages of your story? This kind of pacing has the meter of poetry. It has rhythm. Like this:

*Now all this was done none too soon for already the first part of King Shaddai's army was on the way! On—on—across

---

*From Bunyan's *Holy War*

the plains they came—MARCHing, the four Captains and their divisions—MARCHing, MARCHing, MARCHing—THUNder and SORrow and TERror and JUSTice—MARCHing, MARCHing—TEN thousand, TWENTY thousand, THIRTY thousand, FORTY thousand—MARCHing, MARCHing—on business for the King!

Your audience will see them coming closer, and will squnch back in their seats!

Pacing to slow down without seeming to. Did you ever discover that you were nearly finished and your time was far from up yet? Don't slow down to the dragging point. Speak at normal pace—and put longer pauses between each thought. You will actually be slowing down, but with this kind of pacing, your audience will not realize it.

Pacing to speed up without seeming to. Too much story left and too little time? Speed up by all means, but make your pauses obvious and leisurely between each speeded-up thought. With this kind of pacing, your listeners do not have the feeling of breathless frantic haste. You are making time alright, but they do not realize it.

The Pause

We are not talking about the painful pause of a slow thinker, a speaker who is thinking it up on his feet, but the pause that is put there for a purpose.

Pausing is an integral part of pacing, but it also has a value in itself. The first thing to learn about a pause is not to be afraid of it. Most speakers are afraid of a hiatus—and the more nervous the speaker—the more afraid he is. Afraid that if he ever stops he might lose his listeners, or worse, that he might lose his next thought and not be able to get going again!

A pause adds realism. It makes you more natural, easier to listen to. Incidentally, if your audience is wandering, it is sometimes as startling as a shout. The old joke about the workers in the boiler factory waking up when the machinery stopped, is based on very sound psychology. A sudden silence is an attention-getter.

The pause can create a dramatic effect, add to the suspense, enhance your story in many ways, if you put it to work for you.

Pausing in narration.

> *Diabolus climbed to the top of the tower, where Mr. Incredulity was waiting. They watched the armies marching across the plain for a few minutes.
>
> (*Pause*) Diabolus took the binoculars from Mr. Incredulity without a word, and looked through them, screwing up his face. (*Pause*) He handed them back. (*Pause*) Then suddenly he was galvanized into action. "They look good!" he cried. "They look TOO good!"

This kind of pausing adds realism. The listener is right there with old Diabolus, looking through the binoculars with him.

Pausing in dialogue.

> Ellen: Jane—
> Jane: What—
> Ellen: Did you hear it?
> Jane: (*Pause*) Hear what?
> Ellen: (*Pause*) I heard it. It's something downstairs. (*Pause*) Can you hear it now? (*Pause*) Listen. (*Pause*) Can you hear it?
> Jane: (*Pause*) I did hear something (*Pause*) Yes!
> Ellen: It's getting closer. (*Pause*) It—it's coming up the stairs!

Here again, the listener is listening with the characters —waiting while they make sure they did hear something.

In practicing the use of the pause, you must over-do it

---

*From Bunyan's Holy War

at first. This is to get you used to the sound of silence! After it has become very natural and easy for you, you can strike a happy medium, step your pauses up to normal.

Variety in Your Voice

There is nothing so deadly to listen to as a voice that remains at the same pitch throughout a story, no matter how many shades of feeling the story contains. It is easier to listen to a tone-deaf soloist.

God gave you vocal cords and a voice box to make communication lively and interesting, to convey sympathy, approval, encouragement, pathos, drama, comedy to your fellow-men. Your voice is a wonderful instrument. Use it. Play on it. With the stops in various positions for various effects—muted for sympathy or pathos—fluted for a joy—all pulled out for excitement.

Are you talking about a wicked king? Get it down to ominous. A fairy princess? Use a lilt. A little guppie? Get it up there—guppies are practically microscopic. The Giant Despair? Try mysterioso.

There is no end to what you can do with your voice. Experiment with it. You will find yourself having fun—and your stories will take on a quality of excitement and life they never had before.

To sum up variety: It can be obtained by pacing, the proper use of the pause, and by using variety in the voice. It may make the difference between a colorless story and a story that lives.

The Throw-away Line

The throw-away line is one of the most delicate tricks to master, and that is odd, for we use it constantly in our everyday conversation, without ever giving it a thought.

A throw-away line is exactly what its name implies; it

is to be tossed aside, thrown away. It has nothing to do with the main thread of thought, nor is it of any importance in moving the story or speech ahead. Why then, in the name of common sense, use it at all?

It is used for naturalness. And it works like magic. There is no particular know-how or artistry involved in mastering it; all you need to do is understand the psychology of it, get rid of your inhibitions—and plunge in!

Throw-away lines in dialogue. (The throw-away lines are parenthetical):

Sally: Bill! We've been looking for you all evening! (Is it raining out?) I called the airport and you weren't—(Put your rubbers over there)—you weren't on that flight. (That's alright—just drop them.) You weren't on that flight and mother has been just sick with worry! (Have you eaten?)

Bill: I'm sorry, really. But the most—(Yes,—I've eaten)—the most fantastic happened to me!

Try it. Say it to yourself. Say it as if you were Sally and there was a real live Bill right there in your living room and you were just talking to him. You certainly wouldn't shout at him to put his rubbers over there with the same intensity as you told him mother was sick with worry. Then say Bill's lines as if you were really Bill. You wouldn't announce that you had eaten with the same importance that you announce your fantastic news. You would toss off those throw-aways in an entirely different tone. They have nothing at all to do with the rest of the discourse. They are contrapuntal, like the second thread of melody in music. It is the way we speak in everyday conversation.

Practice throw-aways in dialogue—make use of them. It will make your dialogue natural and far more true-to-life.

Delivery

Throw-away lines in narration. (The throw-away lines are parenthetical):

> He didn't want to go back there. He didn't like the way they did things. He didn't like their attitude. He didn't like— (Well, they didn't like him either. We might as well be honest about it.)

or

> I was double parked and not disposed to loiter. (I also had an account there—you buy things more quickly that way so I told her to just wrap me up one—any one would do.)

Practice throw-aways in your narration too. It will make you delightfully natural and easy to listen to!

The Quick Cue

This takes some doing. But it is worth it. The quick cue is picking up the next line quickly without an artificial pause. It is used only when there is a quick change of thought in narration, as:

> It was then that I felt sorry for my sister Emmy. If she had yelled at me or something—but she just sorta crumpled over like a tallow candle in the desert in August. A man hates to see a woman crumple like that. It's too—(*Quickly*) Boy, what I found out in school next day though sent me to the nearest phone with my last dime!

Or for naturalness in dialogue:

> Stephen: Well, it's Tuesday. We've waited four days, and it isn't going to work.
> Sue: Wait a minute! I have an idea—oh why didn't I think of this before!

Don't wait a minute to say, "wait a minute." If you've suddenly thought of something—out with it! Quickly!

Sometimes it is so quick it interrupts the previous speech, as in this copy from a radio script:

71

Storytelling—It's Easy!

Skipper: Mommy—I'm home!
Mother: (Calling off mike) Bill, is that you?
Skipper: No, It's Skipper. Mother, may I go back to the school library and hear . . .
Mother: (Off mike) Have you seen my pie board?
Skipper: I'm Skipper. Mother, may I go back . . .
Mother: (coming on mike) Have you seen my—where's your father?
Skipper: He isn't here. Only me.
Mother: Have I been talking to you?
Skipper: Yup. Mother, may I go back . . .
Mother: Have you seen my pie board?
Skipper: Nope. May I go back . . .
Mother: Stop and think hard. I want my pie board. Surely somebody must have . . .
Skipper: I didn't see it. (*sudden thought*) Oh. Yes. I had it in the den. I camouflaged it with a scatter rug and made believe it was a bridge. May I go . . .
Mother: Well, if you don't mind, I'd like to camouflage some boysenberries with a pie crust and make believe it's a pie. (*slight pause*) Did you want something?
Skipper: Yup. May I—(*pause*)—now I FORGOT what I wanted!

You have to practice interrupting yourself. In time, you will get so adept at it you will be able to interrupt yourself right in the middle of a word:

Emmy: Mother he knows I've got chicken-pox!
Mother: Emmy, that's a perfectly respectable dis—
Emmy: —It's a *child's* disease!

The last part of the word "disease" never does get said, but the illusion can be so perfect, the listener thinks it did!

To sum up: The art of delivery is an easy one to master once you get it out from behind the professional jargon and explain its mysteries.

The general points of delivery are simply things you knew all the time and just need to be reminded of. The finer points can be mastered—with a little application.

Chapter 8

Narration

Narration holds your story together. It may describe action, bridge time, change scenes, describe scenes, describe people—its functions are many. And it sounds dull.

It needn't be dull. You can make it as exciting as dialogue and as real and alive. You can get variety with it, do tricks with it, play your audience like a harp with it, lure them into avid interest with it. The thing to remember is, there are many different kinds of narration and they serve different purposes. Once you master them, you will be able to draw upon them like tools to create as many different moods as you wish.

Types of Narration

Narration can be in third, second or first person.

Third person narration. This is the most frequently used type of narration and justifiably so. It adapts itself to most stories more easily than any other kind.

> Shorty went to bed but he couldn't get to sleep. He squiggled down in his pillows and looked at the big square of moonlight on the middle of his bedroom floor. It came from the window and had polka dots in it from the curtains. He pretended it was a trap door you could fall through and go down into a dark tunnel where your secret companion was waiting for you. Then he pretended it was the bomb-bay on a bomber,

and you jumped through and counted ten and pulled the cord on your parachute and went down–down–down.

But sleep would not come.

In this type of narration, the storyteller and his audience are discussing a third person.

Second person narration is a "you were there" type. It adds tension and dramatic value and is far more intimate than third person. Daniel in the Lion's Den, in second person narration would go like this:

> You are lowered into the den and the top is closed and you are there alone with the lions in the darkness. At first you cannot see them for your eyes are not yet used to the darkness. You can hear them pacing back and forth, swishing their tails. Then you can see their eyes glowing like coals in the darkness. They come closer and you can smell their foul breath. And your heart squeezes down, for your faith is going to receive its greatest test. Is your God able to deliver you?

In this type of narration, the listener is intimately involved with the story. He is there.

First person (or introspective) narration is the most intimate type of all, for the person speaking is not reporting someone else's story—he has firsthand information—he is living the story himself. It is apt to describe emotion as well as action. It slides in more smoothly with the dialogue.

> I went up the elevator, trying to make up what I was going to say. I knew Millie was bitter; it was going to be hard to face her. Before I could make up anything, a pint-sized nurse whisked me down to a room that said QUIET and let me go inside. She was there, her face turned to the wall, and she didn't turn to look at me. I twisted my hat in my hand and said, "Millie. I–I wanted you to know I'm standing by." I felt foolish.

74

Narration

In this type of narration the speaker is letting the audience in—not only on his actions, but in some stories, on his thoughts.

To sum up types of narration: Narration may be in third, second or first person. Third person is the most frequently used. Second person is the "you were there" type. First person is the most intimate; the narrator is living the story.

Styles of Narration

Narration may be comfortable and homey. If it is not an adventure story, deliver your narration in a friendly warm voice. It is not an earth-shaking report; make it just comfortable.

> Jane and Agatha went down the aisle, got their programs, and were ushered into the best seats. Jane took off her glasses, started to wipe them, decided to leave them off. She gave Agatha's hand a squeeze, and settled down to wait. This was going to be a large evening.

With this type of narration your listeners are relaxed, comfortable, keyed to the mood of your story.

Narration may be tense, low, with quiet understatement. Your story may be very dramatic and filled with suspense but not the shouting kind. You can create tremendous suspense with a low voice—or even a whisper.

> *Mr. Prywell scooted through the hedge, crawled on his stomach up to the cellar window, and peered in cautiously. At first he could see nothing; then he could see the dim outline of their bodies. All of Diabolus' henchmen were there. The light from the candle shot their shadows up the sides of the wall

*From Bunyan's Holy War

and halfway across the ceiling, making them grotesque. He swallowed hard. This then, was the way it would end. They were plotting the destruction of Mansoul. And he could do nothing.

With this type of narration your listeners are waiting, tense, right along with Mr. Prywell, even though you haven't raised your voice.

Narration may be dramatic and excited. If something exciting is happening, show it!

Before anyone could stop him, John ran back across the trestle bridge, the sword in his hand. The bridge was on fire now—the flames leaping thirty feet into the air! The soldiers lined up on both sides of the river and shouted at him to jump —but he didn't hear them—he was an automaton, a flaming running torch—the sword in his hand—running—running—running to his death!

Here your listeners are left in no doubt. This is drama!

Narration may be factual. This is the documentary, or the reporter's type of narration. It is friendly but authoritative and direct and clipped.

In 1884, on a quiet street in Brooklyn, a horse and buggy clattered over the cobblestones and stopped in front of a little white house. It was a well-scrubbed house and had an air of pride about it—and a quiet dignity, and rightly so—for it was the first school for the blind in the United States.

In this type of narration your listener is keyed to the mood of a documentary and factual report. He would be embarrassed for you if you made a dramatic production of it!

To sum up: Narration holds your story together. It need not be dull. It can be most exciting if you master the different types and then use different styles, fitting the type and style of narration to your story. Different stories call for different kinds of narration; with a bit of experimenting you will use the right kind without even thinking about it.

Chapter 9

Dialogue

There is nothing that enhances a story as much as dialogue. Narration sets the stage, but dialogue brings the characters out and suddenly the story has really come to life!

The story of Rebekah can be told as a straight narrative account, but how much more interesting to set the scenes with narration and then let the play go on!

She walked toward the well and—there was a caravan! Suppose it was somebody who had business with her father! She would invite them home and they would have a feast and she would get to dress up and—oh. But such wonderful things didn't happen. They probably wouldn't even speak to her.

And they didn't. She passed them, went down the steps to the well, filled her pitcher, started back up, and then the oldest of them came up to her!

Eliezer: Good evening.

Rebekah: Good evening, M'Lord.

Eliezer: May I, I pray thee, have a drink from thy pitcher?

Rebekah: Ohhhh. Yes, M'Lord. Here.

Eliezer: Thank you.

Rebekah: I—I'll get water for your camels also. Oh no, it won't be any trouble at all!

And she darted back down the steps!

(*You can get them back to her father's house by narration, and then*):

But before they sat down to eat, Eliezer held up his hand for silence.

78

Dialogue

Eliezer: Sire, I cannot eat until I tell you of my errand.

Bethuel: You sound grave. Does it concern our city?

Eliezer: It concerns your household, sire.

Bethuel: My household?

Eliezer: I am the servant of none other than your own uncle, Abraham.

Bethuel: Abraham!

Eliezer: As you know, God promised Abraham He would make of him a great nation. My master sent me here to get a bride for his son Isaac. And not just any bride, sire. A bride from his own people. And he told me to diligently seek God's will in the matter.

Bethuel: And how does that concern us?

Eliezer: I prayed that the first maiden I asked for a drink, and who gave me one, and who offered to water my camels also—that she would be the one. I had no sooner lifted my eyes, when Rebekah smiled at me.

Bethuel: My Rebekah.

Eliezer: Your Rebekah.

Bethuel: Then those exquisite gifts . . .

Eliezer: . . . were for a bride, sire. I have come to ask you for Rebekah's hand in marriage to my master's son, Isaac!

(Back to narration again, until they are ready to leave. Then):

And when the time came to go—

Maidservant: Mistress Rebekah, they are waiting!

Rebekah: Help me tie this, I am all thumbs. I am suddenly terrified!

Maidservant: It is too late to be terrified, they are ready to go!

(Back to narration again, until):

Rebekah: I wonder how far it is yet. I feel as if I have been on a camel all my life.

Maidservant: Mistress, the caravan is stopping. Eliezer comes back to speak with us.

Rebekah: Eliezer! Are we nearly . . .

Eliezer: Mistress, we are near my master's land.

Rebekah: There are men coming toward us—

Eliezer: They are. One of them is my master's son, your husband, Isaac. Here. Let me help you down.

Rebekah: I am down. Thank you. I shall wait here.

And she stood there, tall and very beautiful—and very frightened—and Isaac came toward her. She bowed before him, and he took her hand and they walked along together beside the caravan—into the tapestry of God's weaving—into His will. For God had promised Abraham—"I will make of thee a great nation . . ."

Your narration has bridged the gaps of time, and set the stage for each new scene. In strategic spots in the story, your characters have come to life. And incidentally, it is your characters' speaking that makes the story come to life!

Use dialogue, don't be afraid of it. It will add variety, relieve monotony, make your story really live. It takes practice—and work. Here is how you go about it:

Develop a basic cast of characters.

A little girl	A woman
A little boy	A man
A young girl	An old woman
A young boy	An old man

Then change their voices to fit their characters. What are they like? Are they wicked? Boisterous? Gentle? Kind? Develop their voices accordingly. You will come up with a cast of characters that suit your voice range and your own style. It is very personal, something you must work out for yourself.

Differentiate between characters of the same age and sex with cadence. If you have two children in your story, both girls, both eight years old, change your cadence or rhythm to differentiate them from each other.

Sally: Is it fun to go to Sunday School?
Mary: Sure, it's fun.
Sally: What do you do? Tell me what you do.

Dialogue

Mary: Well—we—ah—sing. And march, and—a—wiggle on our
chairs and—wiggle off our chairs. (*Pause*) And—a—
color pictures. And—say verses.
Sally: Say me a verse!

Sally speaks in a breathless rush of words with little
gasps. Mary speaks with a loping gait; like an eccentric
wheel. They both have the same voice pitch but your
listeners will have no trouble telling them apart. Incidentally, watch out in those gasps for the saliva in the back of
your throat. You can drown that way!

You can apply this same principle to characters of any
age. After awhile you will have no trouble juggling several of them in the same story.

Experiment with your characters' voices. Try tightening
the back of your throat, placing your voice way back in,
without projection. Then try placing it up high and
through your nose. Try projecting it. You can find out
by experimentation how to produce a dozen different
voices.

Practice with your characters' voices. Start out with two.
Make up a conversation between them. Then, like a jug-
gler adding another ball, add more characters to your conversation as your dexterity develops. Make them speak in
quick cues, make them interrupt each other. You will have
the time of your life! After awhile you will become so
convincing, you will have a hard time convincing your
family that you did not have guests in the den.

Try this:

Woman: What did your mother say?
Boy: She laughed.
Woman: She laughed?
Boy: Uh huh.
Woman: You've got some mother.

Practice saying it faster and faster until you can skip from voice to voice with the greatest of ease. It is fun— and yes, after some practice, it is easy!

A word to the men. Do not ever use falsetto for a woman's voice. It will never, no matter how good your intentions, come out anything but comic. For a woman's voice, use a stage whisper with a little volume behind it. It is a "talking whisper" and will serve admirably for a woman's voice. Nelson Olmsted of radio fame, and one of the best storytellers in America, used to occasionally imitate a woman in this way, and it never once occurred to me that he was ridiculous. He was very convincing.

And a general word of warning. Keep your new family of characters for your stories. Don't carry them over into your private life. I backed son number two against the wall once when he was small, and fixed him with a threatening stare. "Stephen," I bellowed—"I cannot have any more of this. We are living on a college campus in a goldfish bowl, and you cannot behave like other children. After this . . ." I stopped. His eyes were twinkling. His face was struggling to keep from laughing. "What's the matter?" I said flatly, the wind out of my sails.

"I can't help it," he cried. "That's your wicked queen's voice!"

To sum up: Use dialogue whenever you can, in strategic parts of your story, using narration to bridge the gaps between scenes. Develop a basic cast of characters. Change their voices to fit their personalities. Differentiate between characters of the same age and sex by cadence. Then practice and practice and practice until you are able to juggle several voices with dexterity.

And don't carry your new dramatic self over into your private life!

Chapter 10

Imagination

A professor in Harvard taught one of the dullest subjects in the curriculum—the law of real property. Now no student in his right mind is going to be able to muster up any enthusiasm for property law. The best he could do would be to resign himself to the fact that this was a subject he had to master to pass his course and put up his shingle. And yet this professor's classes were filled with eager students who crowded in early to get a good seat and waited with anticipation for class to begin. They listened breathlessly while he took a law and traced it back to its origin, inventing characters and dramatizing them. Out of the drama emerged the reason why the law had been made in the first place, what it accomplished and how it evolved into its present form. He took those dusty old laws and made them live again with all the color and drama of an adventure story, and students stood in line to sign up for his classes.

He was using his imagination.

It is so in storytelling and speaking. To take the thrilling story of Joash, the boy king, and merely say that he was kept secretly in the Temple until he was seven years old, is just stating a fact. But it is much more fascinating and exciting to fill in the probable details of those seven years, as in this copy from part of a radio script:

Narrator: And so Athaliah ascended the throne and ruled the land and it was a wicked rule, with the idol of Baal as the official god. Most of the people had turned to Baal—some of the Jews, too—and the ones who did not, attended their own worship in the Temple and gave her no trouble.

What Athaliah did not know was that, upstairs over the Temple courts, in the private living quarters of the Temple priests, the baby Joash was growing up. His aunt, Jehosheba, and his nurse watched over him with loving care.

Jehosheba: Look at him creep—he is like a monkey!

Nurse: Yes, he is very strong—and very bright, too.

Jehosheba: I pray God so. There is much to teach him. Oooh! Watch him! That vase! Joash!

Narrator: And after awhile he began to talk—and to learn.

Joash: (*in tiny boy's voice*): Preserve me—

Jehosheba: Oh, God.

Joash: Oh, God. For in Thee . . .

Jehosheba: Do I put my trust.

Joash: Do I put my trust.

Narrator: And as the years went by, Aunt Jehosheba crowded into his mind everything he needed to know for the great task ahead.

Joash (*in older boy's voice*): Thou shalt have no other gods before me. Thou shalt not make unto thee any graven image or any likeness of anything that is in the heaven above or that is in the earth beneath.

Narrator: And at last the day came when Joash was old enough to understand and be told.

Joash: It must be wonderful to be a king. And rule a country, Aunt Jehosheba.

Jehosheba: Wonderful, dear.

Joash: You've taught me the history of this country so I know it backwards. And of my people.

Jehosheba: Yes, I know.

Joash: If—if this country is worshipping idols instead of God, and the queen is wicked, there ought to be a good king come along and take it over.

Jehosheba: Joash, I . . .

Joash: I wish I were that king.

Jehosheba: Joash. You—you are that king.

Joash: (*after a pause*) You're pretending.
Jehosheba: I'm not pretending. Listen. Listen very carefully
to what I'm going to tell you . . .

That is using your imagination.

Imagination is to take one step beyond the literal verifiable fact. It is to paint a picture—to invent ideas by *seeing*, because to imagine a thing is to *image* it.

Once you get beyond the literal facts and are in the realm of imagination, you feel quite clever and you are even apt to get the idea that you are creating something. The fact is, you are not. No human being ever created anything, even an idea. What you are actually doing is rearranging combinations of old ideas or parts of ideas, and putting them in a new setting. You do not create new ideas, you simply think them out by using the knowledge you already have. Anything "new" that you invent is something that was there, tucked away in your mind all the time. You simply "found" it and pulled it out.

It is reasonable then that the more you see and hear and read and experience and *remember*, the more materials you will have on hand with which to feed your imagination. The conclusion is obvious. Observe, listen, read—and *remember*. Sharpen your senses. Be on the lookout for interesting things—and seemingly unimportant things, too. You never know what will turn out to be a gem, rearranged in just the right combination or put in just the right setting.

Of course, it is possible to become sharply observant, accumulate a wealth of information, and even be highly imaginative, and waste it all because the imagination has never emerged from the passive stage.

Imagination is passive when the thought trend, rather than the thinker, is in control. Here, all your valuable information is dissipated in day-dreaming, in flights of ideas that go round and round and never get anywhere. The material is there alright, but it is never harnessed and put to work.

Determine to use what you have accumulated. If you do not trust your memory, jot it down, carry a notebook, file it away so it will be there when you need it. If you have a multitude of ideas and experiences in your mind or on paper, and practice putting them to use, your imagination will become active.

Imagination is active when the thinker, rather than the thought trend, is in control. Here you are concentrating on your information and on your subject with the idea of making it produce a result.

The more you practice the easier it will become. Seize on any imaginative power you may have and exercise it. Productive imaginative thinking is strengthened by exercise just as muscles are!

Before you know it, you will be able to dip into your memory with the greatest of ease and:

Associate one idea with another.

> Cyrus' men threw their legs o' lamb up in the air *like hats thrown up in an arena.*
>
> The moonlight spread *like a bucket of paint, spilled and spreading.*
>
> The mountains pulled the shadows up over their toes *like blankets.*

Carry attributes of one class of things over to another class.

> The little grubs had snapping-turtles and crabs for teachers, but they were really nice when you obeyed. And sometimes on Saturdays they played Hoppalong-Bassidy.
>
> The mother hen scratched in the barnyard dirt and cried, "Breakfast is ready! Come and get your whole wheat germ!"

Imagination

Fill in probable details.

The wicked king got up, nibbled his royal toast from his royal tray, put on his royal robes, brushed his royal beard, and went downstairs to the conference room.

(Well, that's the way he must have done it. He certainly did not leap out of bed and dash down there to a conference without some preparation!)

Build up situations (Probable effects from known causes)

Rebekah was asked if she would go to be the wife of Isaac and she said, "I will go." (*After she said, "I will go," use your imagination. There must have been a flurry of preparation, she must have been alternately excited and terrified. There must have been a solemn moment of parting. Finish it!*)

Build up situations (Probable causes of known effects)

The five kings of Canaan encamped against Gibeon to besiege it. (*Before you leap to that point, stop and think. They must have had a reason. They must have had a council of war first to decide to go up against Gibeon. They must have been frightened. They must have sat around and talked about it. Build it up!*)

Once you get your imagination in good working order, you will be doing these things without even thinking about it. You will not be consciously "associating one idea with another" or "building probable effects from known causes" or "carrying attributes of one class to another." You will simply be plunging into your story with great glee and observing one general cardinal rule of storytelling: Never state a fact if you can bring that fact to life.

Almost any story can be told merely as a succession of facts. You can leave out all interesting asides and characterizations and dialogue and repeat it as a factual account. But you will be leaving out all the fun!

In Bunyan's Holy War, you might say:

So Diabolus asked Mansoul for Captain Faith. You see, he

knew that if Mansoul lost its faith, he could easily undermine its morale and win the battle. But the mayor refused.

But how much more fun to say:

Diabolus walked into the town, right up to the castle, under M'Lord Mayor Understanding's window and shouted, "Deliver me, Captain Faith! If you will just give me your faith. I'll leave you alone. I'll leave Mansoul to you. I'll never come back to bother you again!"

M'Lord Mayor opened an upper window. "Oh, no you don't!" he cried. "I know you better now than I did before. That last skirmish we had knocked a hole in my roof and let some light in. We'll fight you as long as there's a stone left in Mansoul and a man left alive to throw it!" And he threw an inkwell with careful aim.

Diabolus ducked. "You woke up too late!" he screamed. Prince Emanuel won't forgive you now. You've gone too far!"

"Oh yes, He will!" M'Lord nearly fell out the window in his excitement. "He has promised that whosoever comes to Him He will in no wise cast out!" And he shook his fist.

In the story of Russell Conwell, it is alright to say:

So Russell, as a boy, practiced that melodeon and a lot of other instruments, too, and got to be an accomplished musician.

But how much better to say:

Russell wasn't satisfied with just the melodeon. He peeled bark and sold it to earn a cornet—an uncle gave him an old violin—he got ahold of a cornstalk fiddle from somewhere—he was a one-man band! They couldn't stand him in the house when he began to practice. He didn't care. He took his instruments and went out to the barnyard and played for the chickens. They loved it! They were very intelligent chickens. They sang right back at him! He played his way through boyhood—through high school—through college—until at last he was playing the organ as well as preaching in the biggest Protestant church in the world . . .

Don't merely report that A and B were there and they had this problem and they did such and such about it. We *know* they were there. We *know* there was a problem.

Imagination

But how did they feel about it? What were they like? How did they act? What did they say? Make them real. Make them come to life. They'll stick in your listeners' minds a great deal longer that way.

Never state a fact if you can bring that fact to life!

Follow this one cardinal rule and you will harness your imagination and put it to work without consciously stopping to reduce it to technicalities.

If you are absolutely convinced that you have no imagination and are very timid about launching out into the unknown, all is still not lost. You can find a wonderful substitute for an imagination in reference books. The library shelves are filled with reference books on every conceivable subject—and every book is replete with the most fascinating and little-known information pertaining to almost any story you might be telling.

> Excavators over the Pompeii area found air pockets in the rock. They drilled holes and filled the pockets with plaster of paris and let it harden. Then they carefully cut the rock around the air pockets and lifted it out. When they chiseled down to the plaster of paris they found perfect replicas of people and animals who had perished in the volcano, been turned into a chemical that falls in the salt category—and, down through the ages, dissolved, leaving their likenesses in the rock.

What a choice bit of information to use in the story of Lot's wife along with the conjecture that God *might* have used a volcanic eruption to destroy Sodom.

> In Polynesia there is a myth about a god named Maui, whose mother was about to be visited by the great god Kane. When the hour arrived and she was yet unprepared, Maui climbed a mountain, wove a lasso of cocoanut fibers, lasooed the sun, pulled it down and broke off all its legs. By the time the sun had grown a new set of legs almost another day had gone by and his mother had the extra time to finish her preparations. The long slanting rays of the late afternoon sun are still called "the snares of Maui" in Polynesia.

What an interesting tid-bit to bring out the fact that every corner of the world is trying to explain Joshua's long day!

Reference work will tide you over until you can coax your own dormant imagination into life. And once you realize how fascinating your stories are becoming, you will launch out on your own unafraid. You may have more imagination there than you realize.

It is true that some people are just born with more vivid imaginations than others. The plodding thinker has a harder time rearranging things into new combinations. It does not mean that he is not intelligent. He simply isn't wired for imaginative thinking. He thinks in short straight paths.

The highly imaginative thinker is wired for high voltage by nature. His nerve current flows through his synapsis with the greatest of ease, over a number of paths—producing the maximum number of strange combinations from the given material.

If you do have a vivid imagination, thank God for it and get to work and make the most use of it. If you do not, the reference material is always there.

Incidentally, the insane person is also highly imaginative. The only difference between him and you is that he doesn't know his combinations are weird. And you do.

To sum up: Imagination is to take one step beyond the literal verifiable fact. It is based on knowledge you already have and are able to remember. You can let it dissipate in day-dreaming, or harness it for more vivid storytelling and speaking. If you are not imaginative, the reference books are filled with material to substitute. But you may be more imaginative than you realize. Give it a try!

Chapter 11

Biography

Biography affords one of the richest sources of story material. In biography we rub elbows with people we would never meet in any other way. They share their lives with us, inspire us to bigger things. It's the "if they can do it so can I!" psychology. In the life of many a great person you will find somewhere, if you look for it, that he was influenced by reading the life of some other great; greatness has a chain-reaction.

As truth is indeed stranger than fiction, and a lot more impressive to listen to, you can delight your audiences with strange and wonderful stories of real people—stories that, for inspiration, humor, pathos and sheer adventure, can surpass any fiction that has ever been written.

The secret, of course, is to make them real. Breathe the breath of life into your story and make those dusty pages live again—the streets—the towns—the battles—the homes —the people. Lift your characters out of those books. Shake the dust from them and put them on their feet again —their dreams—their hopes—their feelings—their failures —their triumphs. Lift them out of obscurity. What did they do?

When I was a student I found the study of physiology fascinating. It told me what things *did*. I loathed anatomy with a vengeance. It simply told me what things *were*. I memorized miles of blood vessels whose courses were more complicated than the California Freeways. Naturally, in anatomy class, there was only one thing to do. I learned to sleep with my eyes open.

I was rudely awakened one day by the words "auricular-ventricular bundle of His." The professor had punched it with some emphasis, and it came up out of the drone with ominous significance. He pronounced it "hissss." That was what had awakened me. That, I felt intuitively, would be one we would get on a quiz. I nudged the student next to me. "Bundle of whoose?" I asked.

"Hissss," he hissed back.

"How do you spell it?"

"Spell it? I can't even pronounce it."

I raised my hand. "Doctor, eh, Suture, sir. That bundle. What does it do?" An intelligent question considering the fact that I had been asleep.

"Do?" he said. "Why it's a little white worm-like nerve in the center of your chest. Its function is to stimulate your heart to beat. If it should cease to function for just a few minutes, you would die."

That did it.

I pictured my own little auricular-ventricular bundle of His, busy there, stimulating my heart to beat. It became very real to me. The realization that it had been there all my life, keeping me alive, unappreciated, was overwhelming. "How are you?" I asked it in my imagination. "Are you all right? Do you want anything? A drink of water? A nap? Just let me know. I'll do anything. Just as long as you're happy."

I suddenly loved my auricular-ventricular bundle of His. I had found out what it did, way down there when nobody was looking.

Now, back to our biography—what did these people do? And that does not mean a list of their accomplishments after they became great. What did they do before that?

I was sitting on a platform in a college auditorium once and noticed a plaque on the wall. "You are now what you have been becoming." These people did not leap into greatness over night. They were "busy becoming" all their lives. What were they like while they were becoming?

Some of them were quite ordinary people with a mixture of humor and pathos and strength and weakness.

Just like your listeners.

Some of them got mixed up in unbelievably fantastic plots and lived lives of incredible adventure.

Just like your listeners would like to be.

In either case your listeners can identify themselves with the hero in fact or in fancy. It is all there for them in biography—humor, pathos, exciting narration and dialogue.

> When Fanny Crosby burst into the office of the school for the blind where she was a teacher, she confronted the superintendent with a solemn announcement. "I've started a poem for Daniel Webster. He died this afternoon. Do you want to hear it? I have the first verse written. It's—"
>
> "Wait—Fanny. He didn't die. It was a hoax—to sell papers. I just got word. He is, in fact—Fanny! You look disappointed!"
>
> "Well, I—why no. Of course, I'm not disappointed." Then she dimpled. "My poetry muse is, though. I shall write to Mr. Webster and tell him it was very thoughtless of him not to die when I had already one verse written. And such a beautiful poem!"

Now where, in fiction, can you find a more delicious sense of humor than that?

> When Elizabeth Knox Welch faced the king to ask if her husband could come back from exile and die in his native Scotland, that was no ordinary conversation.
>
> "Whose daughter are you?" asked the king.
>
> "John Knox's, sire."

"How many children did he have?"

"Three, sire."

"Lads or lasses?"

"All lasses."

"God be thanked! If they'd all been lads I'd never have ruled my kingdoms in peace. And your husband is John Welch?"

"Yes, sire."

"Knox and Welch! Surely the devil never made such a match as that."

"Indeed, sire," and she pulled herself up straight. "We never asked his advice!"

Now where, in fiction, can you get dialogue any better than that?

John Welch was a boy who ran away from home, joined a band of robbers, got his bed shot in half with a cannon ball while he was still in it, stopped sword fights in the street with his bare hands, had a ladle of gunpowder shot from his hand and went back and filled his hat with gunpowder and went on to win the battle, and got up out of his death-bed to preach his final sermon.

Stephen Paxon was farmed out as a boy, sent home from school because he stuttered, apprenticed to a hatter because he had a crippled ankle and was useless on the farm, taught himself to read with newspapers, fell in love, married, was lured to Sunday school by his tiny daughter, established thirteen hundred Sunday schools—limping all the way—conquered his stuttering, and became one of the greatest orators of his generation!

A teacher in New York's Hell's Kitchen ran out of firewood and when she was down to the last stick, discovered that the neighborhood ruffians had planned to burn her little school down, come election night, and had already secretly loaded her cellar with crates and planks!

A little Scotch lad addressed a letter to God and mailed it. The postmaster gave it to the town pastor, and the pastor surprised the lad by answering the request in the letter in person!

Biography

Now where, in fiction, can you find more plots with surprise twists—and more adventure—than these!

One morning at a summer conference, two hundred children sat on the edges of their seats as I got to the end of the hour. For twenty minutes the suspense had been so terrific they were ready to burst. I lowered my voice to a whisper:

> Aunt Agnes drew the curtains aside, and gasped, "Johnny, it's your father!"
>
> Johnny stood frozen to the spot.
>
> "Quick! In the closet!" And she pushed him toward the closet door.
>
> "No, Aunt Agnes, let me out the back way. He'll kill me!"
>
> "He'll do nothing of the sort. In!" And she pushed him in and slammed the door. Then she turned and went to the front door to let Johnny's father in.
>
> They sat down to tea and talked about the weather and other things—Aunt Agnes could almost see the closet trembling. Then, with her heart in her throat, she asked, "Have . . . have you heard anything from Johnny?"
>
> Johnny's father stood up. His tea cup crashed to the floor. "Woman!" he shouted. "Don't mention that name to me! I expect he's been hanged as a thief by now. I never want to hear his name again!"
>
> Aunt Agnes held on to her teacup with both hands. She was trembling so she could hardly get the words out. "Oh, I don't know," she said, and her voice was a croak. "Many a lad who has had a bad beginning has had a brighter ending." And then, almost fainting with fright, she called out, "Johnny—come out of the closet!"

And I stopped. The hour was over. There was more to come, but not until the next day.

The children groaned. They screamed. They begged. In mock dramatics, some of them got down on their knees and with outstretched arms pleaded with me, while others swooned against their neighbors.

I left two hundred children speculating wildly on what was going to happen to Johnny. From all reports, that night two hundred children were still talking about it, asking their counselors what they thought. And the next day hoards of them ran to meet me five hundred yards from the camp, with one thing in mind . . .

"Tell us—please tell us—did Johnny come out of the closet?????"

Was this a tale of daring-do from fiction that turned a whole camp into a turmoil of the wildest and most enthusiastic conjecture and suspense? No. It was biography.

And Johnny?

Yes, he came out of the closet and grew up to be one of the brightest lights in the dawn of the reformation. He was John Welch.

Biography is not only a rich heritage for your young people. It is easy to use and dramatize, thrilling to tell, and the supply is limitless. Use it. Apply the same principles of storytelling to it. And open the door to a whole new field of adventure. It can out-fiction fiction!

Chapter 12

Perhaps Your Hero Isn't Human

Although human beings are in great demand as story characters they have not, as many a story book will verify, cornered the market.

Other characters have been doing quite a business, and stories about them make wonderful analogies for children. Animals and birds probably do as brisk a business as any, but sea creatures and plants—and even inanimate things are in on it, too, and doing very well. There is a great host of non-humans that can illustrate behavior, morals, character traits, conduct, philosophy, and just about any other point you might want to bring out.

Once you get started on this possibility, you can get catapulted into other fascinating worlds where there is intrigue and adventure beyond belief.

There is one cardinal rule to remember. If your characters are non-human, humanize them! Give them personalities. Think about them, get to know them, imagine if you can how they feel about the world in which they live, about the lives they lead, about the problems they are facing. Live the story with them. You can actually get to know and feel the emotions of your characters even if they do have four legs, or wings or shells or leaves, as the case may be.

Let's take some copy from a story about sheep:

When it came time to name him, they thought, "If ignorance is bliss, then he must be a blister." So they named him Blister, and the name stuck.

It's a wonder he ever learned anything at all, for when his auntie Mitten told him, "Eat your clover right down to the roots so you'll get your vitamin B and your chlorophyll"— the first word he said was—"Baaaaaaaa."

Now Blister, as you can see at once, is apparently a bit of a problem. Although he is woefully ignorant, nobody can tell him anything. He is, in fact, impossible, and needs his ears pinned back. Once you establish his character, you can proceed to delineate him and make him very real to the listener.

Here's one about some grubs:

Of course, Gregory lived in the nicest section of the pond— in a picturesque old boot, right across from the municipal seaweed gardens which were the pride of the Westside Chamber of Commerce. And he went to private school and had snapping turtles for teachers.

Pete lived on the other side of the seaweed and had crabs for teachers, but they were really nice when you obeyed.

On Saturdays they used to play together. They would sit on the edge of a tunafish can and dangle their feet in the mud. (*Give them feet. Why not?*) And sometimes they played Hoppalong-Bassidy.

"I've got the funniest itch in my back," Gregory said one day.

Here you have two characters, sharply different. Pete has come up the hard way. He is undoubtedly an easygoing simple sort of a fellow. Gregory, on the other hand, has had a more delicate upbringing and many more advantages. As the story turns out he is a curious restless sort, and his curiosity pays off. Your job is to perceive these things and to communicate them to the listener by the characterizations you work out.

Perhaps Your Hero Isn't Human

Let's see how chickens behave:

> Mother Featherneck decided to give them an intelligence test. She said, "Puk puk," and they all said, "Peep, peep," which is baby talk for puk, puk, right back at her. But Quacky and Wacky said, "Quack quack."
>
> "Nooooo," said mother Featherneck. "It's puk PUK. Puk PUK!"
>
> And Quacky and Wacky said, "Quack quack."
>
> "Puk puk, puk PUK, puk PUK PUK PUK PUK!" she cried. I declare, you don't behave like chicks at all."

Anyone with any insight would know at once that mother Featherneck doesn't know she has a couple of ducks on her hands. And that she is a bit of a fuss-budget. Well-meaning perhaps, but a fuss-budget none-the-less. One of those parents who thinks in terms of IQ's and aptitude tests—always measuring her offsprings' intelligence with a yardstick and inclined to fret and worry about them if they do not measure up. Quacky and Wacky obviously have inferiority complexes. If she keeps up this sort of thing she will fracture their futures. Armed with these conclusions, you are prepared to make this little mismatched family into a real drama.

Here is one about some plants:

> Mr. Sun-ripe yawned and stretched his leaves, careful not to make his tomatoes fall off. They were the first tomatoes getting red in the entire tomato patch and he was quite pleased with himself. He looked across the garden at Mr. Carrot and noticed that he still had no fruit. Just a feathered plume, that was all—absolutely nothing to show for all the painstaking care of the gardener.
>
> "Sts sts," said Mr. Sun-ripe, and wondered how they could allow such hoi polloi in the garden.

You can deduce that Mr. Carrot probably does not yet know his full potential—that his roots are his fruits, hidden values of great worth, waiting only to be brought out. And Mr. Sun-ripe is, alas, a bit of a snob.

Even plants can be human!

And a mountain can get into the act:

> Once upon a time there was a mountain who was very sad. Nothing ever happened to him. His peaks were too far up in the clouds to ever see what was going on down in the village where people were living.
>
> Every morning he looked at the rising sun on the peaks in the distance, and every evening he basked in the setting sun on his own snow-covered shoulders. And every day he sighed— "Oh dear. I wish something earth-shaking would happen!"
>
> He might have lived on forever in that state of mind, except that one day, something earth-shaking DID happen. Dr. Henrietta Mears discovered him. And when Dr. Mears discovers a mountain, no mountain can ever be the same again.

Obviously this mountain was longing for fulfillment. To say that he was discontent and ungrateful is not quite fair, however, for he had a glorious destiny, and people of destiny are apt to be a bit restless until it is realized. This particular story happens to be of Forest Home, Christian conference center in the San Bernardino mountains of California, and of Dr. Henrietta Mears who founded it. As Dr. Mears, of Christian education fame, is such a tremendous personality, I could find nothing less than a mountain to put in a supporting role. I made him quite a fellow though—with hopes and fears and a delicious capacity for adventure. He was, however, no match for Dr. Mears. She soon cut his top off, proving that there is a price to pay for a life of fulfillment.

But the point is, even a mountain can be made human!

The possibilities are limitless.

Perhaps Your Hero Isn't Human

Once there was a little staphlococcus who wasn't wanted anywhere, because everywhere he went he caused trouble. It wasn't his fault, really—it was the way he was made. He was just born virulent and nothing could be done about it. It was no fun being a germ.

Admittedly this is a highly unlikely subject for a story. But you see, once you get into the spirit of the thing, there is no limit to what you will think up!

To sum up: Humanize your characters whatever they may be. Give them names, give them voices, give them personalities. Breathe the breath of life into them, and they will become so real to you that you will forget they are not human. If you are convinced—your listeners will be, too.

This type of story makes a wonderful analogy for children or, if you become adept enough at it, you will be able to get away with it for adults, too!

Chapter 13

Music In The Story

Sooner or later you will reach the point where you will be adventurous enough to want to try a little music to enhance your story. It is a good idea, and it can enhance—but it is not without its hazards. If you intend to do it, you should understand the functions of music— when it should and should not be used.

The most important thing to remember is that it must not intrude or attract attention to itself. It is a part of the story, not a solo or a concert in competition.

It can be narrative, comic, foreboding, quick, sleepy, gay, tragic, majestic—and every shade in between. It can either enhance your story or ruin it, depending upon how it is used.

From the beginning of the story to the end, music serves the following functions:

1. As an opening statement, to establish the story-mood and set the scene.

2. As a bridge between your scenes, to serve as a transition. A bridge goes from soft to greater intensity and back to soft before it goes out, slightly overlapping the voice on each end.

3. As curtains to climaxes within the story. A curtain goes from soft to greater intensity

and stays there a few seconds before it goes out.

4. As a "spotlight" to point up a special emotion or action.

5. As a background for either narration or dialogue, to set a mood.

6. As a final climax, a curtain to close your story.

If you are using music throughout your story, it should follow a definite theme that begins in the opening statement, is woven throughout the story, and builds to a climax at the end.

Music as an opening statement. Your opening statement should tell the listener what kind of a story it is.

> (*Music: Gay, tripping mood: Establish and out quickly.*)
> Shorty brushed his teeth in a hurry, combed his hair with his hands, took his frog out of the bottom drawer and put it in his pocket and dashed out to the hall and down the stairs two steps at a time.

You have established the fact that this is a "fun" story. The listener knows what to expect. Here is another example:

> (*Music: Narrative theme: Establish, then under and slowly out.*)
> Once upon a time there was a king who might have lived and died and never been heard of again, except that one day ...

Here you have established a "once upon a time" setting. Your mood is narrative.

Music as a transition bridge between your scenes. The purpose of these transitions is to establish the change and announce a new locale or a passage of time or a new mood. The bridge should be no longer than necessary to adjust the listener to the change. If you are just changing the scene and bridging some time, a simple bridge is all you need.

> Jimmy tucked the letter under his pillow and went to bed. He wondered if he dared to mail it—and if what the postmaster had said was true. It was a long time before he got to sleep...
> (*Music: Narrative bridge and out.*)
> The next morning he walked into the postoffice, the letter in his hip pocket.

If you are changing the mood, the bridge can help you do it. You may go from excited to peaceful:

> All through the night the storm raged, and all through the night they struggled over the mountain pass.
> *Music: Excited, simulating storm, then down to peaceful and out.*)
> In the morning they stood at last and looked over the ridge and down into the valley. The little village was peaceful down there—the storm was over. They began the weary trek down.

Or it may be done the other way around.

> He couldn't believe his good fortune. He pocketed the precious paper, said goodbye to the doctor and started back to the village—
> (*Music: Joyous with melody changing to minor ominous theme, breaking suddenly for:*)
> —But he never got there. For just over the hill . . .

Well, you have prepared your listener for something. There must be at least a giant over the hill.

Sometimes you have several fragments of scenes or bits of narration in quick succession to cover a great deal of time or action by mere suggestion. This is called the montage, and the music bridges simply tie it together.

They should be very brief—a mere suggestion. They may build up to a climax:

> And then began the most exciting summer Ann had ever had in her life. At first it looked hopeless. By the end of the week only two letters had come in.
> (*Music: Swirl up slightly and out*)
> By the end of the second week there were five.
> (*Music: Swirl up slightly and out*)
> But by July they began to pick up—
> (*Music: Swirl up more intensely and out*)
> And by the end of July there were two hundred—
> (*Music: Swirl up more intensely and under:*)
> By August it was coming in bags full—
> (*Music: Swirl up intensely and barely under.*)
> And by September the mail was stacked higher than they could keep up with. It worked! It worked! They had proved it!

Here you have bridged a summer and built it up to an exciting climax. The listener is carried along on the music and bridges this gap with no trouble.

Or it may be the other way around:

> He started up the hill, running for all he was worth—
> (*Music: Treble run, excited*)
> And then he began to run more slowly—
> (*Music: Treble run, but more slowly*)
> And then he began to walk—
> (*Music: Little run, trailing off*)
> And then he began to limp—
> (*Music: Little run in minor, increasing hopelessness*)
> And at last he resorted to crawling. He had to admit Tom was right. The hill WAS a steep one.
> (*Music: Little run in minor, retarding hopelessly and out*)

Here you have started out with enthusiasm and lured the listener from climax to standstill.

Music as curtains to climaxes within the story. Your story may build to several minor climaxes before the final major one. You may want to accent them by minor curtains rather than narrative bridges.

> All night long the people of Gibeon were preparing for the siege. All night long the armies of Canaan were marching across the plains. When dawn came, they had reached Gibeon at last, and Adonizedac cried—ATTACK!
> (*Music: Up Quickly To Climax And Out.*)

Your story does not end here, but reaches a definite minor climax.

Music as a "spotlight" to point up a special emotion or action. Your "spotlight" may be rasping and brisk as a command, or the measured rhythm of a knock on a door, or the steady rhythmic plodding marching feet. It may be minor or weird for fear, or comic and rippling for laughter. It may be as loud as a shout or as soft as a whisper, whichever meets your needs.

If your story contains a repetition of thoughts or phrases that are an important part of the development of the plot, the "spotlight" music to go with them must also be a repetition—a symbolic motif, identifying those thoughts or phrases every time they appear and reappear throughout the story.

Your "spotlight" may be in the form of a music stab. This is used for dramatic effect and is just what its name implies. One note or one chord of music comes in with sudden intensity and diminishes slightly immediately, but without going out. It is like stabbing something and "pulling your punch."

If you are using it simply to accent a sudden thought or mood, it should not intrude but should be kept well under.

Music In The Story

Ellen: (*reading*)
    "Junior character traits." Well, I should be one jump ahead of that one.
    "How to prepare your lesson." I need THAT.
    Let's see— "No lesson should be taught until you have asked the Lord's blessing."
(*Music: Subdued stab well under*)
    Lord . . . I . . . I'm sorry. I've been going at this as if it were arithmetic. I'm sorry . . .

If you are using the stab to accent a sudden highly dramatic turn of events, it can intrude over the speaker's thoughts or voice, or over the action:

    Mother: What was it you wanted to tell me, Kip? You came across the street so quickly—so quickly. And then there was the screech of brakes and the crash of glass . . .
    (*Music: Loud stab in quickly: Sustain few seconds and out.*)

Music as background to color and intensify a certain portion of the story. Always ask yourself—is it necessary? It can enhance your story or, if it is overdone, it can ruin it. It must be inconspicuous, merely guiding the listener's emotional response, not shouting it out. It must sneak in almost imperceptibly and stay well under—not come in suddenly as an intrusion. And it must sneak out as imperceptibly as it came in, unless the particular portion of the story it is under comes to a climax. In that case it should come up for a few seconds and go out.

    Background is usually used under narration. Do not use it under dialogue unless the dialogue is highly emotional, either in a very excited mood or a very sad or nostalgic one.

Music as a final curtain to close your story. This explains itself. Your music simply comes up over the voice at the end of the story, the theme reaches a climax and ends there.

Storytelling—It's Easy!

It is good to understand the functions of music and the various ways in which it can be used, in case you should ever decide to make a real production of your story. However, in the ordinary platform story you will use background music more than any other.

If you should decide to get involved in a production, make sure you know your musician and that you are going to have time for the many hours of rehearsal with him that such a production requires. Remember, you are not just reading a script, you are speaking from memory on the platform—too far away from him to peek at his script. The two of you had better come out even, or your story could turn into a fiasco.

Even for simple background, know your musician. There is a difference between one who plays well and one who plays well and has a feel for mood and can improvise. They are both bona fide musicians; they simply fall into two different categories.

I learned this the hard way. I once wanted the bridges for my story to be fragments of Christmas Carols and asked the musician to use appropriate selections, according to the mood. I gave him the script so he could choose and mark his own selections. Back in those days I was a dreamer and thought all musicians were alike. I was also allergic to rehearsals. I had not yet learned what the professional knows—that the most seemingly artless little ditty, to be done right, requires painstaking labor.

The story began on a note of highest excitement:

> They were trimming the huge Christmas tree at the end of the big hospital corridor. Bill squiggled up on the end of his cot and shouted to the new boy in the next cubicle. "It's Christmas! It's 'most here!!!"

At this highly inopportune moment my musician friend

sneaked in with "Silent Night" in such a slow and reverent way that a shout was almost blasphemous. We struggled on, the music and I—contradicting each other every step of the way. And at the end of the story, when it really got nostalgic . . .

> Bill pressed his nose against the cubicle, and watched her go down the hall. And he thought of what she had said—and how he'd never be afraid again. God was his Father. He was no longer alone, and besides, she'd be back tomorrow . . . and tomorrow . . . and . . . tomorrow.

Now, he came in with a crash and played with gusto and great hilarity to the bitter end—"Jingle Bells," which, as you can plainly see, would have been just dandy at the beginning!

To sum up: Use music with great caution, and only after rehearsal. Understand its functions thoroughly, and where it should and should not be used. Use it only if you are sure it will enhance your story.

And know your musician!

Chapter 14

Your Story On Radio

The first words you breathe into the air-waves have an air of unreality about them, as if, when you entered the vault-like atmosphere of the studio, you had been catapulted into a strange limbo completely disconnected with anything in the world. Is this your audience—the impassive and inscrutable engineer at the control board? Is this your voice, the quavering squeak that does not sound even remotely human? Is this you—the trembling hulk, fumbling ineptly at the rattling script pages? And how can a few little sheets of paper make so much noise?

Your next realization is that something is missing. You would like to establish rapport—but rapport with whom? By the middle of page two you have an irrational desire to throw caution to the winds and shout, "Where is everybody?"

And that is the crux of the problem.

What is missing is that most vital part of the threesome. You are there and the story is there, but the audience apparently is not. You conjure up in your mind a sea of happy faces, and plunge on, raising your voice and using gestures now to break through the wall that is between you.

I mention this because I went through it during the first program where I was completely on my own. For a week I vacillated between thinking of that comforting sea of faces and thinking I was not talking to anyone at all.

Then a letter came from a listener. He was a salesman and he listened on his car radio and his name was McCarthy. After that I talked *to* McCarthy, bless him, and hoped he was not driving under a culvert or in a store making sales while I was driving home a salient point.

In the midst of my friendship with Mr. McCarthy, another letter came. This time it was from a little boy and he listened sitting on a footstool in front of the radio. So then I was talking to Mr. McCarthy and the little boy.

As the letters accumulated, that sea of faces began to recede and I realized that my audience was a collection of miscellaneous people in isolated units. It was a very special relationship—intimate and friendly—not like any other audience at all. The vault-like atmosphere of the studio became unreal and lost its power to terrify. I was in kitchens having coffee with housewives, in living rooms with children and puppies, in cars, in sick-rooms. But wherever I was, I was alone with an audience of one, or at the most, a small group of people.

This then, was the secret of the radio medium. The one-man audience psychology.

It was and it is. From there on out, it is merely a matter of a few rules and technicalities.

Your Equipment

Radio studios vary from simple to elaborate, but basically, a studio is a room that contains several microphones for speakers, sound-men and musicians. In proximity is a sound proof control booth separated from the studio by a large glass window. This control booth is occupied by the control engineer, the director, and odds and ends of strange people who walk in and out, talk and laugh, and throw you into a mild state of shock because you are sure they are talking about and laughing at you.

Your medium is sound. Everything you convey to your listener is done by sound. You cannot rely on facial expressions, gestures, pantomime or props. Words, music and sound effects are your total equipment.

Voice. You are the narrator, setting the stage, describing the action, and keeping the story moving. If you go into dialogue, you are also the characters. The rules for both narration and dialogue apply here. They are described in detail in other chapters.

Sound effects. Some studios have a record library of sound effects. The supply is endless. Crowd voices, wind, waves, storms, thunder, horses, feet running, feet walking, night bugs and frogs, animal noises—there is practically nothing you could want in a story that you cannot find in a good sound record library. This type of sound is operated by the control engineer from the control room and must be described in detail on your script.

Some studios have sound effects to be operated by the sound man right in the studio. There is a variety of them— gongs, door bells, telephone bells, doors to open and close, and often even a "wind machine."

Some sound effects are obvious; some need identifying. A door opening or closing explains itself, but a vacuum cleaner might be disconcerting if you don't mention what it is, either in narration or through one of your characters.

If your sound effect is to set a scene and describe a locality, it is established just long enough for the listener to get oriented, and then brought under.

(Sound	*Night Bugs. Establish and Under:)*
Steve:	Do you have the flashlights?
Bob:	Yep. Here. Do you know the way?
Steve:	Uh huh. Right down this path.

In any event, use your sound effects sparingly, only when you need them, and only to suggest. They should not intrude into the story. It takes the listener only a few seconds to get the idea.

Music. This may be supplied by records carefully selected and the portions to be played, well marked. The records are played by the control engineer from his booth, and brought in and out on cue. You may want to wear ear-phones so you can hear the music; otherwise you will come in and go out on cue. You may rely on an organ or piano—or if yours is a real production—an orchestra in the studio.

Your Setting

Your setting is your listener's imagination. He can go all over the globe and into space; he can bridge gaps of time and space with the greatest of ease, depending on his knowledge and memory for the material. Actually, he can set the stage better than you can. Your job is to merely suggest; don't go in for long, descriptive sprees.

Your Style

Plunge into action at once. And the word to remember is "simplify." Stick to the essentials, avoid lengthy narration, and keep your story moving. Don't strain his patience too far. Remember, he can turn you off!

Your Characters

Again, the rule is: simplify. Keep your characters to a minimum. Keep their speeches short. And keep them speaking! Avoid having one character remain silent too long; he will vanish in the listener's mind and then when he does speak again, will bring the listener up with a disconcerting jolt—"where'd *he* come from?"

In choice of names for your characters, keep phonetics in mind. Avoid names that might confuse. For example, if your script should read:

> First Voice: Who's going to bring the firewood?
> Second Voice: Hugh's going to bring the firewood.
> First Voice: Who?
> Second Voice: Hugh.

You can readily see from reading it aloud that the name "Hugh" has got to go.

Once you have named a character, do not change it to a nickname in mid-script. Stick to the name you began with! And balance your characters' voices so that they are easy to differentiate. If two voices sound too much alike, use cadence to individualize them, as described in another chapter.

Choice of Words

Avoid unusual and "choice" words. They are alright in writing, or even on the platform, but not in radio where you have only the sound of your voice to keep your listener's sustained interest. His momentary dislocation at the shock of a big word may make him miss something important that follows. Remember, if you confuse him you will lose him. He must keep pace with you or he may get behind and never quite catch up again. Once his interest lags, the idea might occur to him to switch stations.

Your Bridges

In reading, your time and locale changes are effected by paragraphs and chapters. In the stage-play, by curtains. In radio, you use "bridges" to transport your listeners to a later time or a different locale.

Music bridges. The most frequently used form of bridge is music. All of the most common forms and uses of musical bridges are covered in detail in another chapter.

Sound bridges. Sound effects are sometimes used as bridges. They are brought up, established, and then brought down under, the same as musical bridges.

> (*Sound*   *Rain and wind, under:*)
> Narrator: All through the evening they got ready for the storm, fighting against time. At midnight it hit in its full fury. . . .
> (*Sound*   *Rain and wind up for bridge and slowly out*)
> Narrator: And at last the long night was over. The morning came, slate-grey and still ominous. They began to survey the wreckage.

Silent bridges. These are often very effective, and are sometimes used through an entire script.

> Bruce: Where'd they go?
> Alice: Bruce, you can't go after them now. Please. (Pause) They went to the station. Bruce, please wait here.
> Bruce: No, I'm going after them.
> (*Sound*   *Footsteps Running. Fade And Out. Five Seconds of Silence. Then Fade In Footsteps Running. Establish And Out For:*)
> Bruce: (Calling Out) Is anybody here?

Your bridges can be any of these types, depending on the needs of your story.

Mike Positions

Various positions and distances from the mike are used to give depth and dimension and reality to the story.

On mike. In this position the speaker is a few inches from the mike. He is there, prominent, on the scene of action.

Off mike. The speaker is some distance from the mike, indicating that he is off at a distance, in another room, not directly in the scene.

Fade on mike. The character starts speaking some distance from the mike and comes in closer while speaking until he has "arrived at the scene."

Fade off mike. The speaker starts "on mike" and fades off, either to indicate the end of the scene or to indicate that he is leaving the scene of action. Fades on or off mike can also be done from the control board. In this case they are described as "board fade" in your script.

> Mother: (*On mike, calling off*) Biff—is that you?
> Biff: (*Off mike*) Yup I'm home. (*Fading on mike*) Sorry I'm late. I just got my graduation ring—you remember my old graduation ring—I got it all cleaned up. Going to give it to—do you know where that chain is?
> Mother: Where 'you going? What chain?
> Biff: (*Fading off mike*) That old chain. It ought to be in my room. (*Calling off mike*) Mom—do you know where —oh, never mind. I found it. (*Fading on mike*) That old chain—how d'you like this? I'm going to give it to Sally—my graduation ring.
> Mother: That's too big for her finger.
> Biff: She wears it around her neck.
> Mother: (*Dryly*) That's too small for her neck.
> Biff: Mom She doesn't wear the *ring* around her neck. She wears it on a *chain!*

Cross fade. One sound goes off while another sound is coming on. The cross-fades can be done with voices, as in the reading of a letter:

> Sally: (*Reading*) Dear Mother: I'm sorry I haven't written before but things have been so busy here, with school underway, and I've been—

116

Cross-fade with:

Mother: (*Reading*) —trying to get my schedule straightened
out, and, and, mother, I hate to ask you this—but I do need
some money. About ten dollars would be enough—

Or they can be done with sounds:

(*Sound: Train Stopping. Cross Fade With Cafe Music And
Crowd Voices. Establish And Under:*)

Segue. A segue is like a cross-fade, only one sound actually
seems to become another, and for a few seconds both
sounds are heard at once. The effect is that one sound
seems to "grow into" the other.

Narrator: And the blind man walked down the hall, groping
tapping with his cane . . .

(*Sound*   *Cane tapping, segue into clock ticking.
Establish and under:*)

Narrator: Every minute counted now. Every minute.

The ticking of the clock "picks up" the same rhythm
as the cane tapping; for a few seconds we hear both. Then
the tapping is gradually gone and only the ticking remains. One seems to "grow into" the other.

A segue has many variations. Music can "pick up" the
rhythm of a voice or a sound, or a voice can segue with
a sound, or two types of music can segue with each other.

Echo. An echo effect is just what its name implies. It
reverberates the sound, as in a large empty closed chamber.
It is used to create the effect of footsteps or voices in a
huge closed space, or for the voice of one's thoughts or
conscience, or sometimes for the voice of Deity. Your
control engineer usually has an "echo" effect right on his
control board, but if he does not, you can simulate the

same effect by speaking across the top of, or into, an empty wastebasket.

Filter. This is done from the control board and simulates the sound of a voice on the telephone. Most control boards have a filter. If yours does not, experiment with holding your nose and speaking. With a little practice you can get a fairly good effect; it's fun trying!

Your Script

This is not merely a story—it is also a blueprint, describing all directions, music and sound effects, too. It must be timed carefully, allowing time for bridges and sound effects and announcements or commercials, as well as the story itself.

There should be several copies in addition to your own. One for your director if you use one, one for the control engineer, one for your musician, and one for the sound effects man.

In writing your script, make it longer than necessary. "Over-write" it with the idea of cutting it down later. An over-long script is often enhanced by butchering, and cutting script down is not difficult, whereas padding a too-short script is not only difficult but awkward and often results in scenes and dialogue that seem contrived.

A rapid "at a glance" calculation for script length is as follows:

Average speed of dialogue is about 150 words a minute.
A line averages three seconds.
Fifteen lines average a minute.

You will time it more accurately later, of course, but this method of rapid calculation will give you some idea of your script length in its rough stages.

After your script is timed and rehearsed, there is still the possibility that you may get off in your timing by inadvertently reading too rapidly or too slowly. In this case your director or control engineer will give you a signal to speed up or slow down. The "speed up" signal is a winding circular motion with the index finger. The "slow down" signal is a pulling apart of the fingers as if stretching something out. In either case, the rules for speeding up or slowing down without seeming to are described in the chapter on pacing. The most comforting signal is the index finger touching or tapping the nose. It means "on the nose"—you are coming out right on time!

To sum up: Radio is a unique medium of sound. Your voice, music and sound effects are your only equipment. Your audience psychology is a one-man affair. You are speaking to individuals and small groups. It is close, intimate, friendly.

You must simplify, get to the point, keep to the point, keep your story moving. Your script is more than a story —it is a blueprint, a work-sheet, describing all the music and sound as well as the story.

Once you understand the one-man psychology of radio and the technicalities of delivery, you will find it a fascinating medium. And that third ingredient—your audience—will be there after all. Your fan mail will soon tell you!

Chapter 15

The Audience

What Is An Audience?

An audience is a miscellaneous collection of friendly glances and gelid stares, interested faces and indifferent yawns, attentive looks and pre-occupied looks and veiled looks. Intense stares and out-of-focus gazes. Humorless eyes and twinkling eyes and vacant eyes.

It can leap from semi-stupor to avid interest in a twinkling. It can remain at rapt attention through a raucous rumpus in the foyer, or become totally distracted by one quiet late-comer straggling in.

It can make you feel assured, foredoomed, expectant, apprehensive, encouraged, squelched, warmed, chilled, drawn out, inhibited, delighted, exasperated, exhilarated with success, weary with despair.

It is candid, non-committal, appreciative, ungrateful, sharp, dull, outgoing, introverted, ingenuous, subtle. It can be warm as a smile, cold as a snub. Critical as a head nurse, tolerant as a grandmother. Eager as a child, bored as a debutante.

It can make you remember forgotten extras, and it makes you forget your best asides. It can enhance your wit with laughter and kill your punch line with silence.

The Audience

It can draw you in a warm circle of friendship or leave you outside battering at the doors. It is, in fact, all the things that human beings are. It is some of these things some of the time and none of these things all of the time. It is as capricious as a summer breeze.

But when it files in and takes its collective seat, and you remember that it came to hear you—you brace yourself and breathe a sigh of gratitude. At least it is there! The best *you* can do is your best. And the worst *it* can do is walk out.

If you always feel apprehensive about an audience—and if it always looks hostile to you—your nerves are playing tricks on you. And you have probably just picked out the wrong faces. A thoroughly hostile audience is practically nonexistent. Completely indifferent ones are rare. So get ahold of yourself. Your audience is friendly and a great deal more in sympathy with you than you realize! Make up your mind before you face it that it is friendly. You will seldom be wrong.

What Type of Audience?

If you have been invited to face an audience and decide you have the courage to accept the invitation, the law of propriety—if not the law of self-preservation itself—should make you find out what type of an audience you are going to face.

Usually your invitation will furnish you with the details, but if it is vague and there is any doubt in your mind, a little groundwork is in order. Make sure of your statistics. What, exactly, is wanted? What is the age group? Is it a mixed audience? If it is a children's meeting, are they very small children? To get a dossier on them is your privilege—and your obligation. They have one on you. You should face each other on equal terms.

Sometimes, even with the best-laid plans on your part, you'll find the rug pulled out from under you because the program committee has made an innovation at the last moment. I have arrived prepared to address teachers and parents, only to be met with an auditorium half-filled with children, and the explanation, "So many of the children wanted to come, we thought we'd make it a family night."

If this happens to you, don't ever communicate to your listeners that they aren't the type you expected, unless you also communicate the idea that you are delighted with the change. If you are not delighted, feign delight until you recover your composure. Be prepared to change your message to suit them, whatever type or mixture they turn out to be.

Where Is Your Audience? (Physically)

Are they scattered? Are they all in the back rows? Are they isolated in little cliques in remote corners, far from each other? Do they straggle in after you have begun to speak? Obviously a compactly seated audience is easier to control. There is not that yawning gulf of empty seats, that feeling of aloofness, that isolated dozer in such plain sight.

If your manner is winsome rather than scolding, you are not out of order in inviting them up front, and they will usually comply. If they do not, drop it in your forgettery and go on as if the subject had not come up. Don't let it discourage you. Simply determine to establish a rapport from a greater distance. Of course if the auditorium is filled, you have no problem. But don't forget to be grateful.

Late comers come in assorted types. Some of them drop unobtrusively in a back seat. Some of them come up front but still manage to be unobtrusive and quiet. Some of them wander about, discuss where to sit, wave to their friends, and, though there are seats on the side, crawl over twenty people to a little spot in the middle too obscure to be discovered by anything but a low-flying helicopter. These are not mean people. They are simply thoughtless people. Ignore them if possible, or if the disturbance is prolonged and warrants it, wait until they are settled.

If you are a member of the audience and the rear-seaters are invited up front, comply goodnaturedly. Perhaps everyone else is afraid to be the first. You may break the ice and the speaker will be grateful.

If you are a late-comer here are some cardinal rules of courtesy:

1. If you enter during any musical selection, especially a solo, or during Bible reading, stand quietly in the back until it is finished.

2. If the speaker has already started, find a seat as quickly as possible. If you like to sit up front, by all means do—quietly.

Even after your audience is finally settled, your problems are not always over. People do a great variety of things, but the four most common are changing seats, leaving, sitting stoically with crying babies and coming down the aisle to deliver an unnecessary message.

I was in the middle of a story once when a gentleman came down the aisle at my extreme left, climbed to the platform, opened the door to the choir-loft behind us, squeezed slowly and painfully through the labyrinth made by disarranged chairs, opened the door on the other side, came back to the platform and delivered a message to the gentleman on the platform at my extreme right. I could not follow his logic—it was like going from New York to Boston by way of Los Angeles. I simply waited quietly until he had finished his errand. The message, it turned out, was one that could have waited until after the meeting.

If you are the speaker remember that these people just aren't thinking. They are acting on impulse, not with malice; they do not realize they are such a distraction. They are doing, in fact, the very things you might do if you had never been a speaker.

1. If your speech is serious, ignore them or wait quietly and in good grace if the disturbance warrants waiting.

2. If your presentation is humorous, you may be able to capitalize on the interruption. For example, a friend of mine was speaking in a hotel ballroom that had a huge staircase leading to an upper balcony and another floor. After he had well begun, every few minutes a small group of gentlemen came down from an upstairs meeting and walked the entire length of the ballroom to an exit at the other end. They were very distracting and the audience was visibly perturbed. When the fourth group came straggling down, my friend said, "Gentlemen, if you would come down and STAY—but you all come down and leave. The psychological effect you are having on this audience is devastating. I'm afraid you will be giving them ideas." The gentlemen grinned sheepishly, the audience roared, the tension was relieved, and no harm was done.

3. If there are crying babies—or one crying baby is quite enough—you must feel your way with the utmost tact. If one starts to cry and it looks as though he intended to keep it up, you might suggest goodnaturedly that his parents would perhaps enjoy the program better from a rear seat. You might stop and give them (parents and child) a long significant look. The baby won't get

it, but the parents may. You might say any number of things from humorous to rude, but nothing you can say after the baby has started to cry is ever quite satisfactory. Actually, the best time to take care of crying babies is before you start to speak, and before they start to cry. There are some speakers who announce tersely at the very beginning, "Crying babies are like good intentions—they should be carried out." This seems a bit brusk. It seems more tactful to announce goodnaturedly at the beginning that if there are any babies present who do not like your speech, you do not wish to impose upon them; they are free to leave and you quite understand. In this way you are not singling out any one baby, and if one does start to cry, his parents can remove him by their own choice. Whatever you choose to say—remember it is the way you say it that counts—say it in good grace!

If you are in the audience remember that the speaker is human. And so are the people around you. You might be more distracting than you realize.

1. After the program has begun, don't change your seat, move about or leave unless you have to. If you must leave early, sit in a back seat where you can do so without disturbing others.

2. If you are the possessor of a crying baby, remember that people for twenty rows in every direction around you are being distracted. Take the baby out, and if he quiets down, stay in the rear of the auditorium with him.

3. Wait until after the program to deliver messages unless they are urgent.

Where Is Your Audience? (Mentally)

Listening consumes nervous energy. When your listeners are absorbing what you are saying, their nerve currents are rushing through their "electrical" system like impulses over a telegraph wire. Only their wiring is a bit different. It is split up in little sections known as synapses with pronged ends and slightly separated from each other. When they are alert and interested, the prongs are close together and the impulses can leap from one synapse to the next as easily as Uncle Tom's little Eva leapt from cake to cake of ice. When they are tired or bored, those prongs pull away from each other and the leap is greater and harder to execute. It is as simple as that. The more tired or bored the listener, the wider the gaps between his synapses—and the wider the gaps, the harder it is to listen.

The odd part is that even if the listener is tired—if his interest suddenly picks up—those little prongs snuggle close again to get the message!

It follows then, that as far as his physical presence is concerned the listener is on his own. But where his mental presence is concerned, the burden of responsibility is on you.

Keeping those little prongs in proximity is your job!

There Is One In Every Audience

There is one in every audience—a person whose facial muscles have frozen into permanent gloom or boredom or disdain or a combination of these.

The first few times you speak, you will be surprised that he is there and wonder why he came. And then you will begin to look for him with horrible fascination—dreading, yet determined to find him. Once you've located him, he draws your eyes like a magnet. As your speech progresses, you will turn to him again and again—seeking his approval, hoping at last you have broken him down. You are bound that you will; he is bound that you will not. There is a deadly kind of combat between you, a war of attrition to see which one can hold out the longer. On rare occasions you can at last break him down and the victory is sweet, but it is not worth the price you had to pay. For in your fierce concentration on him you have lost hold of something in your presentation, something in yourself, and worse, you have lost your rapport with the rest of your audience.

When you see the situation for what it is, it becomes ridiculous. Here you are, perhaps after traveling a great distance, with several hundred people to please and you are letting one face sabotage the evening. You must be free of him. And you can be.

1. Be honest with yourself. What is at stake is your pride. You are upset because one person is glaring in apparent disapproval. Realize that there are probably several more—you just haven't noticed them. And be grateful that ninety per cent of the audience is with you.

2. Remember that you might be misjudging him. Perhaps his feet hurt, or he has chronic dyspepsia, or he is merely concentrating fiercely on what you are saying. I caught a glimpse of myself in the mirror once when I was in deep concentration and I was really frightened. It occurred to me that if I ever saw my face in an audience I would run for cover.

3. Whether his foreboding expression is bona fide or a deceptive mask, recognize him as a saboteur, if only because of the effect he is having on you. Look for him if you must, but only to find out where he is so you can ignore him. Then look for the friendly faces!

I have dealt with him in many guises for years. He followed me from speech to speech—from story to story—always on a different person but always the same face, like a limbless monster in a nightmare. And then one night he approached me after the meeting, thrust out his hand

and with the same expression of doom said, "I never enjoyed anything so much in my life." I shook his hand gratefully. From that moment on I was free of *him*.

It is true, of course, that some glum faces mean just what they say. But no matter what the reason for the gloomy countenance, it is devastating to you if you let it bother you. It will reflect on the job you do, and you will be letting down the ninety per cent of the audience that does like you!

It is not worth it.

To sum up: Your audience is human, friendly, and a great deal more in sympathy with you than you realize. The offenders are few.

You are obligated to this audience from the moment you accept the appointment—obligated to keep the appointment, to be on time, to be worry-free and hurry-free, and to give it your very best.

Chapter 16

Tinymites In A Mixed Audience

I sat in an audience once and writhed in help-less concern. An unsuspecting storyteller was blithely beginning a story to a mixed audience. The grandparents and parents and aunts and un-cles were in the rear. The center was a mixture of in-betweens. The tinymites sat in front. We had already had many—too many—preliminaries. And now, at long last, the story. Happy were we as we awaited the treat with anticipation. Happy was she, as she began. That is just about all she did do. Begin.

"Once upon a time there was a caterpillar . . ."

"I never saw a caterpillar." It was a tinymite in pink organdy with an amazingly shrill voice that came out in excited gasps.

"And this caterpillar wasn't very . . ."

"I never—I never—I never saw a caterpillar."

"Well, you listen carefully and you'll find out what a caterpillar is," said the storyteller. "You see, this cater-pillar wasn't very pop . . ."

The tinymite turned to the boy next to her. "Did you ever see a caterpillar?" she wanted to know. Yes, he nodded solemnly, he had. The storyteller went on.

"This caterpillar wasn't very popular because he . . ."

"My uncle found a caterpillar." Horrors, it was a new

129

voice this time—a boy three rows back. The tinymite turned around eagerly to listen. "—and he put it on our fence and told us not to kill it, and . . ."

"I never killed a caterpillar, but we found a dead bird once on our fence and some boys . . ." a third voice offered to nobody in particular, but by now a teacher had deposited herself in their midst and was busy shushing.

Things were fairly quiet after that, except for pink organdy, who periodically protested the fact that she had been kept in the dark about caterpillars all her life. Nothing short of producing a caterpillar would have administered the quietus, and it was the wrong time of the year for that.

"That," I thought resolutely, squirming in my seat, "will never happen to me." And I wondered just what had gone amiss.

I had occasion to recall that remark with grim humor a few months later. It was in a large church in Boston. The tinymites had been sitting still as long as could be reasonably expected.

It started first like a ripple over a wheat field made by a capricious wind; you could feel the restlessness like a tangible thing. By the time I was called on, they were wandering about at will, carrying their chairs to more strategic spots and standing on them, the better to wave to parents in the balcony. It looked hopeless. With a just-before-you-hold-your-nose-and-jump-off-the-high-dive feeling, I plunged into the story. All was going passably well until I said, "Mother had warned him. 'Don't eat so fast, Shorty, and don't get so excited. You won't be able to sleep to-night.' Sleep? SLEEP? Who wanted to SLEEP? Why to-morrow was CHRISTMAS!"

That was my undoing. A flaxen-haired miss stopped in her flight across the front of the audience and put down her chair. She straightened up and looked me right in the eye. Never have I encountered a more serious face. Like an owl. "Christmas isn't until next Saturday," she said matter-of-factly.

My strategy, after I recovered from the shock, was to go on with the story, ignoring her. I made the mistake strategists far more versed than I have made. I underestimated my opponent. She stood on her chair, the better to set me straight. "My mother knows! Saturday's Christmas. I don't hang up my stockings till Friday night."

I tried a new angle. "In this story, we're pretending tomorrow's Christmas," I told her confidentially, bending the mike over and purring into it just for her. That settled it for awhile. Of course, I had one up on her. I was on the stage and had a mike. But the damage had been done. She was settled. I was not. I was off to a bad start and never quite recovered. I remained unsettled to the bitter end.

That was many stories and many mistakes ago.

What had gone amiss? Is it impossible to tell stories successfully to those nursery and kindergarten children—the tinymites?

No.

It is easy if you follow a few simple rules. Remember:

They cannot concentrate from a distance. It is absolutely impossible for them to bridge the gap between themselves and a figure far away on a platform. Even if they are in the front row, the figure is still high in the air, remote, not

131

connected with them. Their nerve impulses simply have not graduated to that stage of accomplishment yet. They should be kept in small intimate groups if possible and not brought into an auditorium with a mixed audience.

I have often offered to tell the tinymites a "special" story first, getting right down there in front of them, and then have them marched off to their graham crackers and little games. Or I have offered to stay an extra half hour and go off into their department where they were having their own little program. There I would squnch down and draw them around me in a circle and we would have our own story, as nice as you please, some of them coming close with affection, circled in my arms—some of them distant, rapt and wondering. Some of them wandering off. But at least they were in their own element, their little nerve impulses not straining to leap from synapse to synapse, to comprehend something too far away. And we were happy.

If you are planning a program, you will do well to keep tinymites by themselves. If you are the storyteller, and the audience is mixed, offer to tell the tinymites a "special" story first or spend some time with them separately. If neither of these solutions is possible, you are in for it! Aim your story at the tiniest tinymite. Plan to please the youngest and count on the indulgence of the older ones. And even then, you'll have your ups and downs.

They cannot concentrate for long. Their listening span is only a few minutes—the tiniest ones, only two or three minutes. It is amazing how much you can say in three minutes if your story is planned and organized to a standstill. I auditioned for a radio program once and had to ad lib for one minute on a subject that was just handed to me cold, and I found out that even one minute can be a long,

long time. Why, I had said everything I could think of at the end of thirty seconds! In three minutes you can get more across to tinymites with a well-planned and well-told story than you could in fifteen minutes of rambling. The trick is preparation.

They cannot concentrate when they are tired. Tired to begin with, that is. If they are in their own little group, the story is, of course, put in a strategic spot, right after they've been doing something—not after they've been sitting primly on their chairs for fifteen minutes while all two hundred of their wiggle muscles are saying, "Let's GO!"

If they are in an auditorium with a mixed audience and they have gone past the time they are capable of concentrating, their minds will seize on any stray thought-trend that captures their fancy and follow it with a tenacity that is unbelievable. Remember the caterpillar.

What to do? If you're the storyteller, ask to have teachers at vantage points to administer the quietus. If you are in the audience, slip into a seat beside the offender if possible. Sometimes the mere presence of an adult will do the trick. If you are the program-planner, in the name of good programming and enjoyable listening, put your storyteller on an early spot!

And now for the story itself.

No program planning can rise above the story itself. It must be good. It must be custom-made for tinymites. It is easy to take most stories—even the great majestic stories of the Bible—and custom-make them for the little ones, if you remember:

They learn with their senses. Their senses are the windows of their souls. They love to feel and smell and touch and listen and see vivid pictures.

They are fanciful and imaginative. There is no limit to where they can go and what they can do in their imaginations. There is no limit to what they can pretend. And they love to pretend!

The younger tinymites pretend in little ways. Don't stretch their imaginations beyond the pale of their experience. Your sentences, incidentally, must be "little" too.

> The first day Jesus went to church—he was a tiny baby.
> He was!
> His mother, Mary, wrapped him in a blanket.
> His father, Joseph, got the donkey ready.
> And two tiny birds in a cage.
> He rode on the donkey with his mother.
> She held him carefully.
> And Joseph walked alongside.
> The donkey went clippity CLOP. Clippity CLOP.
> When they got to church, the first one they saw was—an old man.
> His name was Simeon.
> Simeon said, "May I hold baby Jesus?"
> And he did.
> Then they were all thankful.
> Simeon thanked God for letting him see Jesus.
> And hold Jesus.
> Mary and Joseph thanked God for letting them have Jesus.
> And the two little birds?
> They were left at the church as a thank-you gift for God!

And you "wrap" and "put birds in a cage" and "hold the baby" and "walk alongside" and "see" and "hold" again! And bow your heads to thank God.

That is all the tiniest ones can stand.

For older tinymites you can enlarge a bit. But remember you still have to use your imagination. It is alright to start with, "Now, boys and girls, a long time ago, God made the world we live in." But how much more fun to say:

Tinymites In A Mixed Audience

Let's pretend your mother's mixing cake in a bowl. It's chocolate. You can smell it. And she spills some on the table and you walk by and—quick-get-a-finger-full-and-run-run-run-RUN! Right out to the back porch.

It's the first nice day of spring and you sniff the air and it smells GOOD. (*Pause. They'll sniff. Wait and see.*) Look! Look at the trees! They have little tiny leaves on them! (*Get your voice up there. Any tiny leaf worth mentioning to a tinymite is mentioned in a squeak.*) They didn't have leaves a week ago. How do you suppose that happened? (*They'll want to know and you are ready for an earth-shaking pronouncement*). They didn't just happen. They were made. God made them. Just like mother made the cake. He made them according to a plan. Just like mother made the cake according to a recipe.

I don't know about you, but I can FLY. Yes I can! (*You might tell them here to watch out for their chocolate—it's dripping from their fingers. They still have their chocolate coated fingers. Stuck up straight. When I tried it, all the little girls licked their chocolate back up their fingers so it wouldn't drip; the little boys did not.*) I just give my feet a little push and—up—I—go! Are you still pretending? Well, give your feet a little push. Don't look down! Make you dizzy. Up—up—up.

Now. We're up here way above the world, and we can see it the way God sees it.

In the beginning God made the world. He hung out the moon—and He hung out the sun—and He hung out the stars— and the stars sang together for joy. Yes, they did! Says so in the Bible. And He hung out the earth. Little bit of a thing way down there. And on the earth He put . . . (*You can put on the earth what their attention can take. Make it brief. Short sentences. And make it vivid.*) . . . "Great big trees (*full voice with appropriate gestures*) and middle-sized bushes (*normal voice*) and little tiny flowers (*high voice*). And animals! Great big bears (*full voice*) and middle-sized dogs (*normal voice*) and little tiny mice (*high voice*). And fish! Great big sharks (*full voice with appropriate gestures*) and middle-sized goldfish (*normal voice*) and little tiny guppies (*high voice*). And water! Great big oceans (*full voice*) and middle-sized rivers (*normal voice*) and little tiny brooks (*high voice*). And when it was all done—it was just right. He made it according to a plan. Just like mother makes a cake. Just right.

135

I have told this story and had tinymites holding chocolate fingers up straight, licking them off, pushing their feet to fly. And without commotion. They can go worlds away right there in their seats. I confess their captivation and cooperation and comprehension was unbelievable. I also confess that after one telling, a little boy asked me how we got back down. I'd left them up in the air! No matter how you plan, they'll think of something!

Both of these stories are for tinymites. For the younger ones, the facts are there—without embellishments or detail. For the older ones, a bit more detail can be added. But they both do the same thing. They let the little listeners see and feel and taste and smell and hold. And they both appeal to their imaginations.

And you? You are warm and friendly and intimate and close. Like a mother hen—drawing them into your confidence, into the circle of your love—into the circle of God's love. And their little nerve impulses are skipping away with ease. You haven't strained them a bit!

To sum up: Tinymites cannot concentrate from a distance, or for long, or when they are tired. They learn with their senses and their imagination knows no bounds. The story should be short and vivid—all unnecessary details weeded out.

It is ideal to keep them by themselves in small intimate groups, but if they are in a mixed audience get down there close to them and aim your story at the tiniest one.

Admittedly there are times when tinymites must be in a mixed audience—there are occasions when it is good parent-church relationship to have them there. On these occasions the preliminaries should be cut to a minimum and the storyteller put on an early spot!

Chapter 17

The Speaker Is Coming

The speaker is coming.

The reactions are varied and interesting.

"Miss Ballpoint is here. At the hotel. Just checked in."

"Who?"

"Our speaker. For tomorrow night."

"What's she doing here today?"

"Got in a day early. What'll we do with her?"

"Do we have to do something with her?"

"Well, she'll think it odd if we don't. I'm tied up with the Auxiliary this afternoon. I wondered if you could take her around to see the town."

"I can't. I'm going to make my cookies for the tea. I'm room-mother and . . ."

"I wonder if Emily could do it?"

"She has Brownies. (There is a painful pause.) All right I'll do it. I'll bake my cookies tonight. What's her number?"

"Oh, Alice, thanks. If you'll do that, we'll have her for dinner and the evening and I'll try to get somebody else to take her for tomorrow."

And so, at great inconvenience, gracious people take Miss Ballpoint over, careful to see that she does not have one dull lonely moment alone from the time she arrives until she steps upon the platform. And at great inconvenience, Miss Ballpoint goes along with it all. Unhappily, she would rather be back in her hotel going over her notes or writing long overdue letters or washing her hair.

"Miss Spinayarn writes that she will arrive Tuesday and wants a reservation at the Welcome Retreat Motel."

"Nonsense. Tell her we'll have her in one of our homes. I've already asked the Shumysters if they'll take her. They have four children. She does children's work. She'd probably adore that. She doesn't want to be in any old motel."

But does Miss Spinayarn want to be in a motel? Yes indeedy, she does. Any old motel! She's been averaging four hours sleep a night for weeks on her heavy itinerary. And she is, at the moment, too exhausted to adore children except in the abstract. Given a badly needed ten hour's rest, she'll be ready to adore them in concrete examples.

"What'll we do with Doctor Wastebasket? He insists on staying at the Solitude Hotel. He's already in."

"But I cancelled his reservation there yesterday! The Gaynes' wanted him at their place."

"The Gaynes? Do they have enough room?"

"They were going to put him in with their son. They thought it would be such a good influence. For their son, I mean."

"Well, he's already at the Solitude. He said he had an important writing deadline to meet."

"Well, I suppose we'll have to let him stay there if he's already in. The Gaynes can have him over for the evening and we want him tomorrow in the afternoon to show him the new gymnasium and after he speaks tomorrow night we've planned a little get-together . . ."

And there, unless he is a hearty character and adept and diplomatic at saying "no," goes Dr. Wastebasket's deadline.

This is a sad waste of everybody's time and energy. The tragedy is that the speaker is not the only one who suffers. The well-meaning gracious people who are taking care of him suffer, too. They often take care of him at great inconvenience.

What is wrong? Are all speakers aloof and introverted, wanting to be left alone in an ivory tower to emerge only during their presentation and disappear again for further meditation? Do we just leave them all alone as a matter of course, to play safe?

It is a problem. Happily, there is a very simple solution. The trick is to realize that speakers are not all alike. For every speaker who wants to be left alone, there is one who longs for fellowship, would love to see the town, and would welcome the opportunity to stay in a home and sit at the kitchen table for a cup of coffee.

And because behavior is dynamic, no speaker in either category feels exactly the same way all the time. The speaker who generally wants to be alone might suddenly want fellowship. And the one who usually wants fellowship might suddenly need to be alone. It depends on his itinerary, how much work he is trying to do enroute, how much sleep he has had, how he feels.

The most diplomatic way to solve the problem is to give him a choice. Tell him there's a reservation at the hotel—or the McNamaras would love to have him if he feels so inclined. There's a new library and a view from the mountains you'd love to show off but only if he feels he can spare the time.

Who knows? Miss Ballpoint might not want to write

letters or wash her hair. Miss Spinayarn might adore being with the children. Dr. Wastebasket might not have a writing deadline and might be longing for fellowship. But do give them a chance to tell you before you make plans for them.

Without putting it into words, we separate speakers from other people in our thinking. We think of them as some sort of merchandise being delivered to our town, leaving the audience in a state of excitement or a halcyon glow or a state of bored indifference, as the case may be, and being promptly dispatched to the next place.

A man who was going to introduce me to a club asked me about my family. "We don't like to think of speakers being mailed to us in a box, speaking, and then being put back in the box and mailed to the next place," he said. "We like to know they're human."

Of course.

They are human, subject to different moods, and sometimes tired. No two speakers are alike, and no one speaker is the same at all times.

It is an act of delicacy to "feel them out," find out which arrangements they would rather have, and give them a feeling of freedom to be frank with you in making a choice.

In discussing the pros and cons of this little problem we must not forget that the speaker himself has a definite obligation. The gracious people who are trying to take care of him have problems of their own. Their invitations are sometimes made at great inconvenience. Even if he cannot accept, he should be grateful that they cared to bother. They are not just an audience. They are people, too.

Chapter 18

Anything Can Happen

If you have arrived thus far in this book, it is hoped that you have given the technicalities of rhetoric and dramatics at least a cursory reading and that you intend to go back and study them point by point until you have mastered them all. The various intricacies of putting a story together and the art of delivery with all its ramifications are purely academic and you can master them if you will. If you have absorbed the practical advice sprinkled generously throughout, you are one step ahead of the academic and well on your way toward that comfortable state of mind and body known as "disciplined relaxation." These things are tangible; your mind can get ahold of them.

We are now about to deal with still another realm that is very difficult to define and in which it is impossible to lay down specific rules. It is the realm of the unforeseen and the unexpected. As a storyteller or speaker, there is one mysterious phenomenon you must be prepared to cope with from the start. It is that, no matter how much you have studied or how carefully you have prepared, emergencies arise that are not covered in any of the books. It is like the baby who swallows the page that tells you what to do if he should swallow something.

At first you will think that unexpected things go wrong because you are a novice. After a few years of speaking you begin to realize that these emergencies are always just around the corner, always new and different. Or, if they repeat themselves it is invariably with a new twist so you have no precedent to fall back on. You just have to use your wits, keep your sense of humor, and remember that, all things being equal, you will survive.

This chapter is a miscellaneous collection of unexpected things that have happened. Some of them were actually turned to advantage; others left the speaker in a mild state of shock for days.

They are in no way an attempt to teach you anything, but merely presented for your amusement, and to prove that one great axiom of public speaking—ANYTHING CAN HAPPEN. And without warning. It is what makes the speaking interesting.

It Can Happen Before You Begin

My cab pulled up in front of a small New England church one winter evening many years ago. I was on time and at the right church. I had rehearsed my message carefully. All my mental indicators pointed to a safe landing. I had never heard of an "Anything Can Happen" department, so naturally it was a surprise to see a woman at the curb in the stance of a relay-race runner—one hand pointed to the church, the other outstretched waiting to grab me the minute I paid my fare.

"I've been trying to reach you all afternoon but you did not answer your phone," she accused, which immediately put me on the defensive and I was no match for her from that moment on. She brought out all my guilt complexes. I let her grab my hand and run me up the walk.

"We had to make the whole dinner an hour earlier because there's a game at the high school tonight and everyone wanted to go to it. I tried to let you know . . ." she ran me through the foyer, past the heaped-up galoshes and down a flight of stairs. I followed her meekly, examining myself to uncover my motives in ruining the evening of these good people.

". . . Anyhow everybody has left for the game," she went on, "except for a few people I persuaded to wait to hear you." She ran me expertly around a bend in the corridor. I examined my past to uncover the reasons why I was such a wretched failure.

"So just do your story—and do make it short. They are all so anxious to get to the game!" She swung a door open. Around the deserted tables were about fifteen people, their faces drawn in lines of longsuffering about to expire.

Like most cowards do when they are cornered, I said something completely irrelevant. "May I take off my hat?"

"Nooo," she hissed. "There isn't time."

"My galoshes?" I wailed, like a child determined to win some minor point even though the major skirmish is lost. She didn't even bother to answer that one. It was too unworthy.

"Here she is," she told the fifteen martyrs, and nodded to me with a glint in her eye that betokened real trouble if I made a break for the cloakroom. There was nothing to do but plunge into the story—hat, galoshes and all.

To say that I did not have a sense of liberty and rapport with that audience is putting it euphemistically. My mind was numb and my thoughts were shackled; I think my voice was reedy though I did not really hear it. In fact, it is quite possible that I might have started the story with "Once upon a time there was a game." At any rate my mind turned off and I finished the story on automatic pilot. The next thing I remember, I was huddled in a cab, bound for the railroad station. I do not even recall

143

if I made it to the cab on my own steam. Of one thing
I am sure however—I did have my hat and galoshes on.

At a suite in the Waldorf Astoria in New York, I sat
at the head table contentedly munching my cherry pie
and carrying on a lively conversation with the gentleman
next to me. The audience was composed of radio station
managers and owners, and there were to be several speakers
after lunch. I was one, and quite happy about it, until my
dinner partner picked up his program, glanced at it and
put it down with a terse "This is going to be dull."

"Probably," I agreed, hoping he would drop it there.
He did not.

"In fact," he went on, "these speakers look so dull, I
suggest we skip out right after lunch. I'll take you back
to Philadelphia."

"I can't," I croaked hoarsely, "I'm one of the dull—eh—
one of the speakers."

I remained shaken for days.

One night I had chosen to sit in the front row until
called upon. After the introduction I made my way briskly
to the platform. The step was high. Vaulting it was not
too difficult, but what followed will forever remain a mystery. How it was accomplished I simply do not know.
I flipped through the air like a rocket and landed in a
sitting position with one shoe off. It was a feat of gym-
nastics I thought anyone my age was incapable of per-
forming. The audience did not know whether its speaker
was dead or alive. There was an audible gasp of horror
and concern. Two gentlemen quickly leapt to the platform and lifted me to my feet. I perceived two things
at once. I was not hurt in the least and the faces looking
at me were so horror-struck that I wondered if it would

be possible to ever break the ice and get off to a good start. I propped myself against the podium, put the shoe back on, and said drily, "Now I can't begin this speech the way I'd planned to. I was planning to say, 'Don't things get dull sometimes?'" The audience roared with sudden relief and release of tension, and we were off to a better start than if I had not made such a striking entrance.

It Can Happen After You Get Started

One of the quickest thinking speakers in America is Bob Ringer, humorist and sales consultant. One night he was speaking at a dinner-club. It was one of those over-programmed evenings, and to save time they had introduced him while waiters were still clearing. As he rose to speak, a flustered waiter hastily removed somebody's untouched strawberry shortcake, and in doing so, dumped the entire concoction—strawberries, whipped cream, ice cream and cake on his shoulder and down his tuxedo shirt front. There was a horrified gasp from the audience. Bob just stood there, looking down at his shirtfront. Then, unperturbed, he picked up a spoon and began scraping it up. "Well, it looks like . . ." he drawled, ", . . it looks like, tonight the dessert's on me." The audience absolutely howled with relief and delight. He proceeded with his speech as if the incident had never happened. He had turned a horrifyingly embarrassing incident into an asset.

I spoke to students once in the recreation room of a college in New York City. They had improvised a platform by placing two doors over saw horses and covered it with a huge rug. I was well into my discourse and in the middle of a sentence when the doors suddenly separated, the rug formed a hammock, and I was lowered unceremoniously, nearly out of sight. There was a scramble while they pulled me out and mended the damage to their platform. The student body remained ominously silent during the operation; it was considered a catastrophy and they did not know how the speaker would take it. They were silent and apologetic as I climbed back on. I said briefly, "Booby trap," and went on with the sentence that had been interrupted in so novel a manner. The students roared with delight. No harm was done. In fact, it did me good; I had an even warmer audience from then on!

At a summer conference once I was in competition with, of all creatures, a mouse. He crept cautiously along a window-box at the high windows behind me. The audience on the whole could take a mouse in its stride, but there were a few to whom he was a matter of great moment and utmost excitement.

"There's a mouse!" cried one little boy, announcing its presence to any adult who might be missing the finer points of the show. The result was the undivided and audible attention of the audience on the mouse, who was greatly encouraged. He flipped, he whirled, he skipped and danced. The heady excitement of audience approval had transformed him in one mad moment from a shy little field mouse into a diva. And I confess I was bitten by that dread green-eyed monster, the bug-a-boo of all the platform world—jealousy of a fellow-performer.

There was nothing to do but put him in his place. I said as much to the audience. "That mouse," I reasoned to them, "is a permanent resident. He can perform here all summer. I am here for only thirty minutes. It is only fair that he retire and give me the platform." Whereupon I took my notes, gave him a gentle nudge and sent him scurrying into oblivion. "I hope I have not discouraged him at the very beginning of his career," I told them, "because for a mouse that has never had any platform training, he shows great promise." And I went on with my presentation in peace.

The audience had been brought under control—but good-naturedly and with tact. I saw no need to waste any tact on the mouse. He was an incorrigible upstart and deserved what he got.

Your Audience May Leave

In a state-wide PTA convention, an entire day was set aside for speeches by radio station managers and performers representing various types of programs. I was not scheduled until late in the afternoon. The audience was bone-weary. While my introducer was busy, it dawned on these worn-out people that the next speaker was going to discuss Christian programs and tell a story. They decided that this was one they could skip. En masse, they began to depart. Rows of them, literally hundreds of them made for the rear doors of the huge ballroom.

I made a quick and desperate decision. This was no time to discuss Christian programs; these people needed a jolt. I leapt to my feet and plunged into my story. I chose the most exciting introduction to the most exciting story I had. The people piled up at the door like a row of dominoes that had been tippled. They stood, listened and decided to stay. I thanked God with one part of my mind while I went on with the story with the other part. Some of them sneaked back to their seats and the rest of them stood in the back of the ballroom listening intently. After I finished the story and knew I had their complete sympathy—I launched into the very briefest discussion of Christian programs!

Storytelling—It's Easy!

You May Have To Lock Your Audience In

At a rally attended by two thousand children—I was unhappily scheduled late in the program, after preliminaries that were the equivalent to a full-sized program in themselves. Everybody who had "said a few words" felt burdened to give the message of the day. By the time I was put on, those children had had just about all they could stand. One little girl decided she wanted a drink. She crawled over fifty others in her row, started up the aisle and whispered to an usher. The usher nodded yes. The message spread as if by native-drums and the desire for a drink spread like measles. Before I could get my first breath and launch the attack, the aisles were crowded with departing children. Recessing them all for a drink was impossible; it would have taken an hour. There was nothing to do but ask the ushers to stop them. They were settled down again in ten minutes and I made my story five minutes long. Though I had short-changed the committee that had brought me there, I felt a greater responsibility to a captive audience that had already been held captive too long and to the parents who had already been waiting forty minutes to pick up their offspring and were crowding into the back of the auditorium.

Carry On

To those of you who have never branched out into platform speaking these things might seem exaggerated. Those of you who have braved the vagaries of the speaking world know that they are not. You could undoubtedly match them with more colorful tales of your own experience.

The point, as you have probably already guessed, is that practically any emergency, no matter how wild, can be turned into an advantage. It can almost enhance your performance rather than ruin it, if you seize the opportunity with good nature, keep your wits and sense of humor foremost and push your ego into the background.

If it is an emergency that cannot be turned to advantage and there is nothing for you to do but go on somehow, remember that you will be bruised and battered only temporarily; it is merely your ego that has been hurt anyhow—you will survive.

Just be ready for anything. Because as long as programs are launched and speakers are speaking—ANYTHING CAN HAPPEN!

This chapter is not intended to discourage you. The case histories have been set forth knowing that you are human and therefore incurably optimistic. It is assumed that you will read them, perhaps chuckle a bit, and agree —"Of course, anything can happen—but it's not going to ever happen to me!"

This is what keeps us going.

Chapter 19

These Things Need Not Happen

Mr. Boise entered the building, loaded down with equipment. The chairman was waiting for him in the front hall.

"How do you do?" said Mr. Boise. "May I put these things somewhere?"

"I'm Davenport," said the chairman. "You can set them right here for now. We're ready to serve. Been waiting for you."

They went into the banquet hall, up to the head table, and the evening began. The meal was excellent, which was fortunate, as things turned out.

The program began with community singing. The song sheets contained enough to make up a fair-sized book, but the songleader was up to it; not one was left unsung. The announcements became so involved they achieved the stature of a business meeting. A string ensemble took on the proportions of a miniature concert. The soloist who followed was really excellent. It wasn't until the third number that the law of diminishing returns began to operate. The toastmaster was in fine form. He had copious material to bridge the gaps between numbers. In addition to his prepared material he was good at extemporizing. One thing always made him think of another. He was also a man of impulse. When he spotted Mr. and Mrs. Youngston, recently returned from Indo-China, he generously invited them to say some words about their trip. They did, quite a number of words. Mr. Boise did not hear them, however. He was negotiating to get someone to sneak his equipment surreptitiously in and leave it by the side wall.

It was while the quartette was singing its second number that Mr. Boise glanced at his watch. It was nine forty. He leaned over to the chairman and whispered, "How much time do I have?"

"Oh, take as much as you want," the chairman smiled. "We have all night. You're on next."

It turned out happily that he was.

The toastmaster began a panegyric, filled with lovely things Mr. Boise was, and worthy deeds he had done, and sprinkled with lovely things Mr. Boise was not, and worthy things he had not done. At last he came to—

"And now I give you Mr. Boise . . ."

Mr. Boise slid to the edge of his chair.

". . . Who is not just a local celebrity . . ."

Mr. Boise started to rise.

"There is no north in him . . ."

Mr. Boise got back on the edge of his chair.

"There is no south in him . . ."

Mr. Boise settled back. He was no sage, but he knew there was east and west to come.

". . . There is no east in him . . ."

Sure enough.

". . . There is no west in him."

Mr. Boise slid to the edge of his chair.

"He—is—ec—cu—MENical!"

There was a solemn pause. Mr. Boise waited for an "and now—Mr. Boise." There was none. The toastmaster, it turned out, was through. He had exhausted himself. He did not have one more word left in him. Mr. Boise, at long last, was on.

The first problem was the huge portable podium that was on the table. Mr. Boise was too short to stand behind a podium without a riser, and besides his presentation did not lend itself to podiums. It required a set-up of a different nature. He was a chalk-talk speaker with a built-in background of sound and music. He had brought along his own tape recorder.

Of course, it took awhile for the tape recorder to be set up and plugged in, but the chairman did that with the help of the boy who went to find an extension cord while Mr. Boise set up his chalk-talk apparatus.

He began by modestly disclaiming all the extra things the toastmaster had sprinkled in and then got to the presentation.

The chalk-talk went passably well. Of course, it would have been easier for Mr. Boise if the other occupants of the head table had already moved aside instead of nudging each other and moving aside piece-meal. And it would have been easier on the audience if there had been a light in front of Mr. Boise and his accoutrements instead of those glaring lights behind him on the wall. And it would have been easier at the end for all the people to get their aching limbs in motion again to leave if only Mr. Boise hadn't taken the chairman's "Oh, take as much time as you want" remark seriously. And if only the toastmaster hadn't got his second wind after the chalk-talk and rehashed Mr. Boise's message and mentioned some of the things it reminded him of, and topped it off with some more announcements he had just remembered.

It is highly improbable that all of these things would happen to one person or on one program. But it is conceivable that you, either as the program chairman or speaker, might make some of them. I confess to being guilty of making one or more of them at some time or other. The fact that I never made all of them at once is probably because I never had the opportunity. Viz. I have been guilty of arriving late but never ran the gamut of Mr. Boise's comedy of errors because I didn't carry a tape recorder and chalk-talk apparatus. I simply wasn't equipped to do the job as thoroughly as he did. Let's go back over this fiasco and put the blame where it belongs.

First, Mr. Boise entered the building loaded down with equipment.

The point is not that he entered the building loaded down with equipment. The point is, he should have entered the building loaded down with equipment at least a half hour earlier.

If you are a speaker with no more props than the notes on your cuff, get there on time.

If you are a speaker with props, "on time" means early. A flannelgraph board should be set up, the backgrounds and figures in proper order so they will go on with ease and right side up. Chalk-talk equipment should be completely set up and fumble-proof. Tape recorders and sound effects should be ready, in good working order, pre-tested, foolproof. Blackboards should be requested in advance, set up and ready with chalk. Test tape recorders, sort out flannelgraph figures, send somebody for chalk. Don't set up after you are called on!

Second, the program began. Here the blame is two-fold. The chairman should have timed the evening, controlled it in the planning stages, and kept it under control. Mr. Boise should have found out ahead of time how the program was arranged, whether other speakers and announcements were eating into his time. He should have made it known ahead of time that he needed room and suggested that the head-table occupants be asked quietly to move before he started to speak.

If you are the speaker make a list of your needs, make them known by phone or mail beforehand, and arrive early enough to see that they have been carried out.

If you are the program chairman:
  Control your program.
  1. Time your program carefully, ruthlessly slash it if it threatens to be too long.
  2. Resist the temptation to add extra participants because they have been suggested and are available.
  3. Keep announcements down to a minimum and make them interesting.
  4. Find out what is needed for your speaker—podium, equipment, microphone, lighting, and have it set up. If he has not thought to do this, the burden of responsibility falls on you.
  5. Give each participant an allotted time. Explain to him that the program can be just so long, that you have just so much time for preliminaries. That's all there is, there isn't any more.

  Control your toastmaster.
  1. Give him a schedule with the preliminaries worked out so the speaker will be put on at a specified time.
  2. Anticipate that he might get carried away and prepare to avoid it. Prearranged signals are good; they can be agreed upon in a good-natured and friendly way before-

hand. Then if you must curb his enthusiasm, you can save your program without losing his friendship.

Third, Mr. Boise Was Introduced. The blame here is partly on Mr. Boise. He should have done a little ground-work beforehand. And he should have refrained from commenting on the introduction. The bulk of the blame, however, must be placed on the toastmaster. He had already gone over his quota before he ever got to the introduction. He was talking on borrowed time; he should have borrowed more frugally.

If you are the speaker, see that pertinent information gets to your introducer ahead of time and make it brief. From that point on, you are at his mercy. You may be introduced by superlatives. If you are, do not apologize or disclaim; make no reference to it. You may be introduced by an over-long speech. In this case there is nothing you can say without being rude. You may be introduced in such a way that you scarcely realize you have been called upon. Or by the wrong name. Or with your name mispronounced. Or as a singer. Or without warning. Or not at all. In any case, take it in good grace, ignore it, and get on with your message.

The choicest introduction I ever got was at a banquet in Los Angeles. I had been sent there by Forest Home, a large Christian Conference Center in the San Bernardino mountains. I was introduced as "Ethel Berrett from Forest Lawn"—which is Los Angeles' famed cemetery. Hardly an introduction calculated to get a speaker off to a lively start.

If you are the introducer, use that pertinent information in as interesting a manner as possible. Get the name correct and make sure ahead of time that you know how to pronounce it. And be brief, but not so brief he does not realize he has been introduced. I've been brought up short in the act of swallowing coffee with the words "and now, our speaker" that dropped like a bomb-shell and nearly finished me off.

A friend of mine told me he had once been introduced with: "It is now my privilege to introduce the speaker so he can speak, which I have done and which he will do." In all fairness to that particular introducer, it had been done with a twinkle, in good humor, and the audience and my friend were delighted.

If you are talking on borrowed time and your introduction must be that brief, the real point is how you do it. By your manner and your voice, you can be gracious and courteous and let the audience and the speaker know you are glad he's here!

Fourth, the Speech was on. At last. Here again, the blame was two-fold. The chairman should not have said, "Take as much time as you want," and Mr. Boise should not have listened. They are generous words, gracious to say. They make you feel so expansive. They can also ruin your program. They are welcome words, lovely to hear. They go to your head—make you feel so wanted. They can also dull your judgment; heeding them could be your undoing.

If you are the chairman, control your speaker.

1. Give him an allotted time. He can conceivably give you as much trouble as anybody on your program.

2. Give him enough time to warrant his coming. Balance your program to give him the bulk of it. If he was worth inviting, he is worth that consideration.

If you are the speaker, control yourself. Once you are on nobody can stop you. The responsibility is yours. Don't be misled by a polite audience. Remember a mustard plaster exhausts its efficacy in twenty minutes. You can leave it on all day but it will just lay there. It isn't doing any good.

Your presentation might be anywhere from twenty minutes to an hour, depending on what category it falls in and what your audience came to hear. Just don't exceed your efficacy quota.

Fifth, the program was over. Except, that is, for the anticlimax—the rehash of the message and the added announcements. The time to avoid this was beforehand, but of course, Mr. Boise wasn't there beforehand.

If you are the speaker, remember that the fellow who follows your message can ruin you. Does your message end on a serious note? Do you want the evening to end there with a simple dismissal to avoid losing the impact? Do you want the message followed by an invitation or a challenge? If so, do you want the person closing to give it? All of these details can be ironed out tactfully. If he is new at the job, he will probably appreciate your suggestions. If he is stubborn and a man with ideas of his own, at least you have tried. I have never yet encountered a program-closer who was not amenable to suggestion.

If you are the program-closer, never rehash the message or say it reminds you of something and launch into a speech of your own. Simply thank the speaker and close. If an urgent announcement has come to your attention, make it quickly. If the speech has been serious, make it quietly and with dignity. Then close!

The difference between a program that is out of control and blunder-ridden and a smoothly run program that is so good the audience is surprised when it is over and does not know where the time went, is simply good organization and foresight.

If both speaker and chairman anticipate the program pitfalls they can be avoided; none of these things needs to happen!

Once a program is out of control, it is too late for anything but resignation.

Chapter 20

You Will Have Setbacks

I put son number one on a train in Philadelphia one September evening and bade him a fond farewell.

"Goodbye, mother," he said bravely in a high squeaking voice. He was going away to Florida to school.

I picked him up at the same station the following spring and he said, "Helooo, mother!" in a deep bass voice. He was a foot taller and his sleeves came up to his elbows. He swung his luggage up with the greatest of ease and followed me in long strides to the car. He helped me in with great ceremony. He did all the talking. I was speechless.

I was still speechless as we drove up an almost deserted Walnut street in the darkness, when I spotted a diner open. This young man, I thought, needed a cup of coffee. And I needed a better look at him in the light; he might not even be mine!

We pulled up in front of the diner. He swung the car door open for me. He swung the diner door open, too. Indeed, if the booths hadn't been screwed to the floor he would have swung one out to seat me. He was loaded with new manners, much erudition and lots of poise.

He was still discoursing learnedly with his new booming bass voice on the beauties of the trip up from school when the waitress came along, fixed him with a gelid stare and said, "What'll you have, sonny?" It was a crucial moment.

"I'll have a hamburger," he began—"with onions and . . ." his voice wavered . . . "ketchup and . . ." it broke . . . "all the trimmings." It went up in a high squeak. He was right back where he started.

So will you be, on occasion. A bad day, a case of nerves, a flash of self-consciousness and all you have learned will waver, break and go up in a high squeak.

The things that might trigger this off are legion. You might be thrown by distractions or embarrassed by interruptions. Or be discouraged by seemingly indifferent audiences or seemingly ineffective presentations. Or be periodically plagued by the feeling that after you finish your next thought your mind is going to go blank (it seldom does, but just thinking it is going to is enough to make you feel as if you had carried a trunk upstairs). You might suffer all of these things and more, and if you do, be tempted to give up the whole idea and leave storytelling and speaking to the other people to whom it comes easily.

That you must not do.

Remember that you cannot learn to be a full-fledged finished storyteller or speaker all at once. You can learn the fundamentals *almost* all at once, but it takes practice to work them out. It is like typing. The touch system can be mastered in a short time; you can train your fingers to "see" the keyboard in a week or two, but it takes many months of practice to acquire the skill and confidence that are necessary to make an expert typist. It is so in anything worth mastering.

Actually, an occasional set-back is good for you. It tempers your confidence with the right kind of humility. To misquote the bard:

> "His attitude was humble, sweet and low,
> An excellent thing in speakers. . . ."

At any rate, just don't let setbacks discourage you. We never really lose what we have learned and practiced. The secret is to use each setback as a stepping stone; learn from it, profit by it and go doggedly on. A good storyteller and speaker gets that way by keeping everlastingly at it!

Acquiring storytelling ability might be slow, but it is fun and it is easy. And this little guide-book with all the detours and rough spots and bad weather posted, should reduce your pitfalls to a minimum.

Chapter 21

You Or Your Message

There is one last question. Which is to be remembered, you or your message?

I was introduced to a new girl in the art department of Gospel Light Publications one day. She looked up from a delightful sketch she was working on. "Do you remember speaking at the Long Beach Civic Auditorium?" she asked.

"Several times."

"I mean the time you told a story about a girl named Ann who . . ."

"Oh, yes. I remember that."

"I was in the audience. You know that story made an impression on me that I'll never forget. It practically changed my life, but . . ."

"I'm glad. But what?"

"I don't know how to tell you. I was telling Betty about it—I remembered the story, but I didn't remember who told it. I told her it was just 'some woman' and she told me it was you. You know—" and this came out in a rush— "even though I've seen you around here for a week, I still didn't know you were the one!" She grinned sheepishly. "I didn't want to tell you but Betty said you'd be glad to hear it. I think it's an awfully rude thing to say."

"No." And I grinned back. "It's the most rewarding thing you could say."

And it was. The story had been remembered; I had been lost in the shuffle.

Once at a speakers' table, I got involved in a conversation about a speaker who had preceded me the month before. "He was wonderful!" my host exclaimed.

"What did he talk about?" I inquired politely. It was the wrong thing to say.

"Why he talked about . . ." he turned to the man on his right. "Frank, you remember the speaker last month?"

"Oh, sure, tremendous!"

"What did he talk about?"

"Why it was . . . let's see now. Wait, Doc Harvey will know." He called up to the end of the table. "Bill, remember last month's speaker?"

"Oh, yes—terrific personality!"

"What did he talk about?"

"He . . . well, I can't remember, but he was great!"

It is only fair to that speaker to add that in a moment they did recall his subject and it was excellent. And in fairness I must also admit that often—all too often—(even once is too often) people have not been able to recall a thing about some story they have heard me tell.

The point is, that as a speaker you may be remembered for yourself or your speech, or both, depending on you and the nature of your presentation. There are some speakers who are so delightful to listen to it doesn't matter much what they say. It is always good even though it may take a little doing to recall what it was. They are "tremendous personalities" and they give an audience something just by being there.

This is not true of storytellers, however. A story, if it

is to fulfill its purpose, ruthlessly demands the center of the stage so its characters can come to life and have their being. You as a storyteller must make a choice.

This, if you have followed all instructions, is not going to be easy to take. Now that you have practiced all the ways and means and know all the tricks—most of them you must forget. At least you must forget them as such. And in time, you will. They will become a part of you, and you will not be conscious of them as techniques—they are just you. But a newly developed and disciplined you, lifted to a higher plane of artistry. And the day will finally come when you realize that there is not room on the platform for both you and the story; one of you has got to go. That will be the day when you forget yourself completely, lose your identity in the story. You ARE the story.

It is the highest form of art.

After I finished the story of "Gregory the Grub" one time, a woman rushed up to me. "I completely forgot you were YOU!" she cried. "To me you WERE a grub!"

Oh well. The choice isn't always easy.

Acknowledgements

Eleanor Doan of Gospel Light Publications looked over the first rough draft of the manuscript and gave me many valuable suggestions. The other people who helped me with this book did so many years before it was written. My mother stood alone in her faith in me during the years when I could not cross a room without falling over my own feet. My sons not only listened with avid interest to my stories, but by their antics, furnished me with a rich source of story material. Dr. Herbert Mekeel of Schenectady encouraged me to tell Bible stories. Dr. Howard Ferrin of Providence encouraged me to put them on radio. Jack Wyrtzen of New York encouraged me to put them on television. Stanley High of Readers' Digest encouraged me to "always be writing something—never let yourself go stale." Joan Wise Jesurin of McGraw Hill Book Company gave me valuable criticism in writing. Dr. J. Palmer Muntz of Buffalo, valuable criticism in platform propriety . . . . to mention a few.

Each of them contributed in one way or another, to the writing of this book. I heartily thank them all.